YOU CAN DO IT!
PUNCTUATION

Andy Seed and Roger Hurn

Hodder

Many thanks to Barbara Seed for acting as consultant on this book

First published in Great Britain in 2011 by Hodder Children's Books

1

A Catalogue record for this book is available from the British Library

ISBN 978 0 340 93119 6

Book design by Fiona Webb
Project editors: Margaret Conroy and Polly Goodman

Printed and bound by CPI Bookmarque Ltd, Croydon, Surrey

The paper and board used in this paperback by Hodder Children's Books are natural recyclable products made from wood grown in sustainable forests. The manufacturing processes conform to the environmental regulations of the country of origin.

Hodder Children's Books
A division of Hachette Children's Books
338 Euston Road, London NW1 3BH
An Hachette UK Company
www.hachette.co.uk

YOU CAN DO IT!
PUNCTUATION

Contents

Meet the Odd Mob

The Odd Mob is a gang of seven friends – a right rabble of different characters, some cool, some clever and some clots. A quick 'who's who' will tell you what you need to know.

Wozza

Lowdown: questions spin round her head like socks in a tumble dryer.
Likes: question marks
Dislikes: all other punctuation
School report: she loves asking questions – it's a pity she's hopeless at answers.

HMD

Lowdown: this heavy metal dude is the Mob's seriously hairy 70s rocker.
Likes: carrying a guitar at all times, even in the shower.
Dislikes: peace and quiet
School report: a bright pupil whose classic wide-legged stance has greatly improved this year.

Max

Lowdown: Max Mullet is tough, keen and adventurous. Oh, and she's magnetically attracted to trouble.
Likes: having the worst hair in the solar system.
Dislikes: being poked in the eye; liver and fashion
School report: Maxine is very popular, especially with headlice.

Ulf

Lowdown: half-boy half-beast, Ulf is not only as daft as a brush but looks like one.
Likes: grunting, and doing anything which is a naughty no-no.
Dislikes: soap and ballet
School report: shouldn't he be in the zoo?

Flash

Lowdown: the fastest girl on the planet, always in a hurry.
Likes: trackies, trainers and treadmills
Dislikes: waiting
School report: English 14%; Maths 9%; Science 11%; PE 253%

Googal

Lowdown: she's so bright her teachers have to wear sunglasses.
Likes: complicated sums
Dislikes: easy listening
School report: if she was any sharper we could use her to cut cheese.

Deej

Lowdown: so cool he makes cucumbers jealous.
Likes: drum 'n' bass
Dislikes: triangles
School report: the brightest thing about him is the bling he wears.

Shagpile

Lowdown: a carpet, with a tail at one end and a cold wet nose at the other.
Likes: bones, bottoms, lamp-posts
Dislikes: cats, postmen, vets
School report: Tail wagging: great; Barking: loud; Biting: useless; Hungry: always

Mr Sumo

Lowdown: a rude wrestler and big bully who is the gang's evil enemy.
Likes: sitting on people
Dislikes: children, old ladies, baby animals and being fair
School report: expelled for eating the photocopier.
(Not one of the gang.)

You'll also meet two of the Mob's mates, Cheesy Chad and Multiple Joyce, from time to time – they're fun and full of top tips too.

What's It All About?

A quick quiz:

A) Do you enjoy reading punctuation books at school? YES/NO
B) Do you read them when you don't have to? YES/NO
C) Do you only bother with punctuation when you have to pass a SATs test? YES/NO
D) Do you think punctuation's really boring? YES/NO

If you answered NO for questions A and B and YES to questions C and D then CONGRATULATIONS, you're a normal kid! And you're smart. You learned how to speak English. And did you need a teacher to help you figure out how to do it? No, you didn't. You learned it when you were a baby, which is pretty amazing.

OK. You're great at learning stuff so why do you need this book? Here's the answer. You're already smart but this book can make you smarter at punctuation. It's like having an extra brain you can keep in your pocket – only not so squelchy. And you don't have to go to school to read it either.

Questions you won't find answers to in this book

How do you know when you've run out of invisible ink?
Are crop circles the work of cereal killers?
If your glove's too big does it still fit like a glove?
What do sheep count when they can't sleep?

So what IS in this book?

Help to avoid embarrassing situations like this:
Teacher: The punctuation in your homework is terrible!
You: Well, don't blame me.
Teacher: Why not?
You: Well, it was my mum that wrote it.

So, as Cheesy Chad says ...

If you want to find out more about punctuation – read this book.
If you want to meet the Odd Mob – read this book.
If you want to impress your friends with a load of jokes – read this book.
If you're shipwrecked on a desert island and are starving hungry – eat this book.

If you also need help with spelling and grammar, there are two more Odd Mob books to sort you out. Remember, You Can Do It!

How the pages work

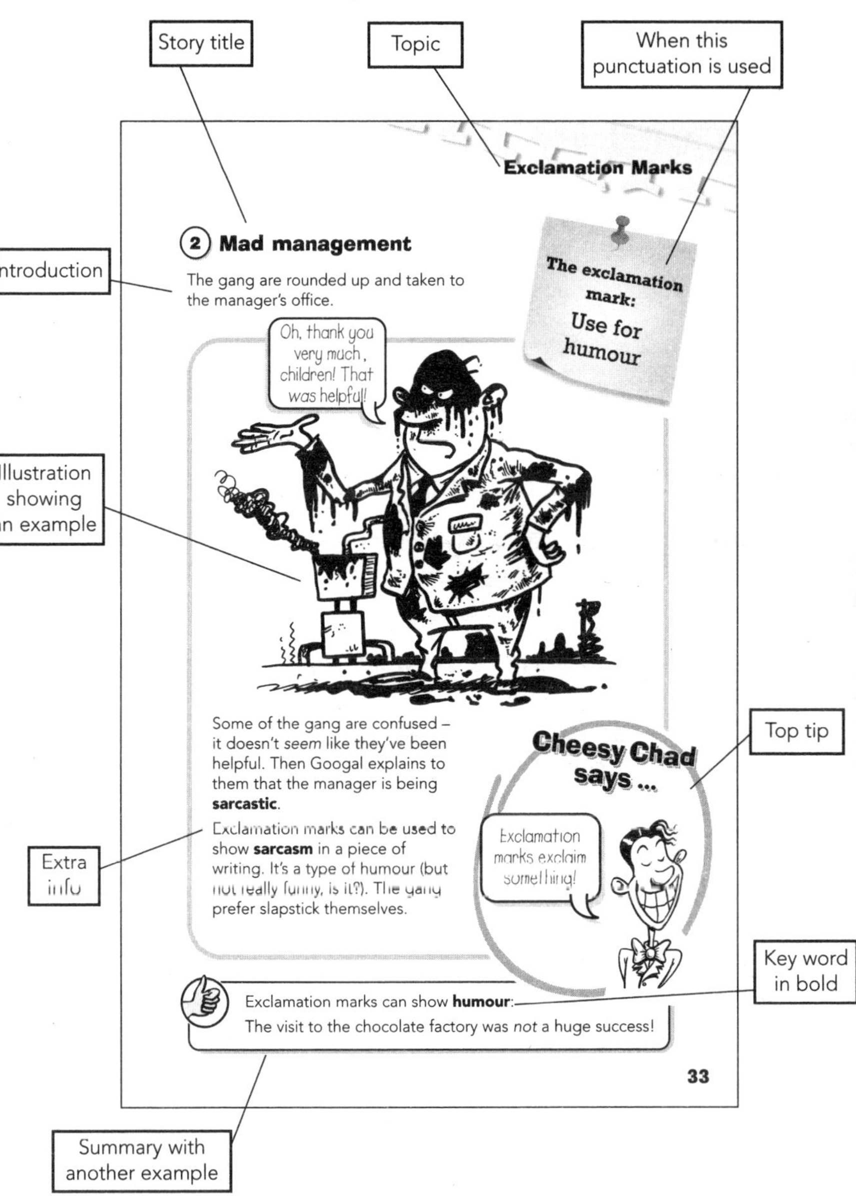
Story title
Topic
When this punctuation is used
Exclamation Marks
2 Mad management
ntroduction
The gang are rounded up and taken to the manager's office.
Oh, thank you very much, children! That was helpful!
The exclamation mark: Use for humour
llustration showing in example
Some of the gang are confused – it doesn't seem like they've been helpful. Then Googal explains to them that the manager is being sarcastic.
Exclamation marks can be used to show sarcasm in a piece of writing. It's a type of humour (but not really funny, is it?). The gang prefer slapstick themselves.
Top tip
Cheesy Chad says ...
Exclamation marks exclaim something!
Extra info
Key word in bold
Exclamation marks can show humour:
The visit to the chocolate factory was not a huge success!
33
Summary with another example

Capital Letters

Holiday Time

Capital letters:
Start every sentence

1 Capital idea, old chap

The gang are planning a holiday together, but they have been told they can go only if they improve their written English – especially **capital letters**!

That night they are all online using messaging …

New Message

New Attach Find Font Print Send

Max:	i am soooo excited about this holiday.
Googal:	Well, you'd better start using a capital letter for the word I if you want to go.
Deej:	we could go to a tropical island!
HMD:	You won't go anywhere unless you start your sentences with a capital letter!
Flash:	What about a whitewater kayak holiday in New Zealand? sounds cool to me.
Googal:	It does sound cool but you missed the capital S for Sounds – it follows a question mark.
Wozza:	What's a kayak?
Ulf:	What's a holiday?
Shagpile:	Woof!

Start every sentence with a capital letter:
You always use a capital for the word '**I**' too. **D**on't forget!

2 Names, names, names

So, it's decided. They're going camping

in Wales.

Wales! But what about the tropical beaches?

What about New Zealand?

Capital letters: Use for people's names

We can't afford it. It's camping in Wales or nothing.

Why are we camping in whales – what about all the fish?

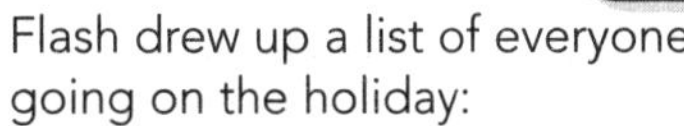

Flash drew up a list of everyone going on the holiday:

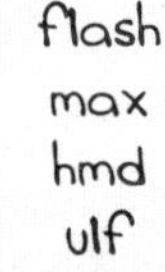

flash	Flash
max	Max
hmd	HMD
ulf	Ulf
wozza	Wozza
googal	Googal
deej	Deej
shagpile ✗	Shagpile ✓

Whoops – she forgot that people's names need capitals.

Not coming:
Mr Sumo

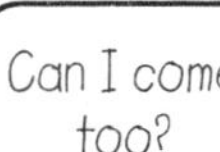

People's names always begin with capital letters:
Deej **M**r **S**umo **S**ir **I**saac **N**ewton

3 The place to be

The gang are finally heading off on holiday …

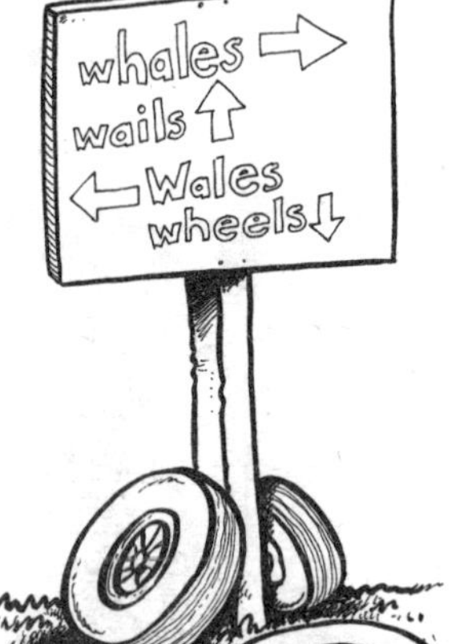

Which way now?

It's left because countries, like other places, always have a capital letter.

The gang are soon lost again …

Where's Llnnfgfg Campsite?

That way. Turn left at Mold, right at Rhyl and cross the River Clwyd. It's only 185 miles.

Many **names of places** need capital letters:
UK **C**alifornia **Y**ork **N**ile **L**och **N**ess

④ Something about a title

The gang stop for a rest. To pass the time they play charades (you know – that daft acting and guessing game).

Capital letters:
Use for titles

It's a book! Something to do with swimming.

James and the Giant Beach?

I fink it's a song – is it Land of Hope and Breaststroke?

No!
It's a TV programme. And it's two words: Blue Peter!

Blue Peter? What's that got to do with swimming?

Use capital letters for the **titles** of books, films, plays, songs, TV shows etc:

The **C**hronicles of **N**arnia   **S**hrek   **A**utumn **D**ays

Capital letters: Use for organisations

(5) Loitering within tent

At last the gang arrive at their campsite and put up their tents.

Max got her tent from a shop, **F**lyaway **C**amping.

Deej got his tent from the **S**ea **S**couts.

Googal got hers from the official tentmakers to the Queen, **L**eakie & **T**awn.

Ulf got his tent from the **US A**rmy.

HMD got his from **K**ent **P**olice.

Flash and Wozza are sharing. Their tent came from **T**he **P**ound **S**hop

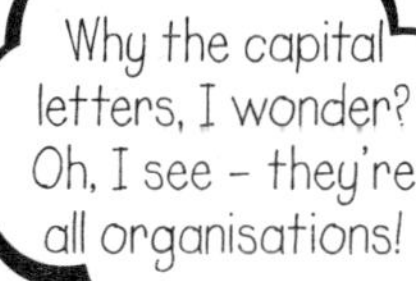

Why the capital letters, I wonder? Oh, I see – they're all organisations!

Joke Break

Doctor, doctor! Please help my sister – she thinks she's either a wigwam or a marquee.

Oh, not to worry, she's just too tense.

The names of **organisations** need capital letters:
Channel 4 **A**ston **V**illa **FC** **E**ton **C**ollege **T**esco

6 Don't forget to, right?

Capital letters:
Use for days and months

The gang's camping holiday is in full swing. They decide to send some postcards – it's a good job Googal's checked them …

Dear Mum and Dad,
It has been snowing since ~~tuesday~~ **Tuesday**. Are you sure this is ~~july~~ **July**?
Well, at least the holiday has a nice ~~christmas~~ **Christmas** feel.
Love, Max

~~friday~~ **Friday** 1st ~~august~~ **August**
Dear Uncle Dolf and Auntie Olaf,
The weather is good – plenty of blizzards. A bear came into my tent last night. It was delicious.
See you at ~~easter~~ **Easter**.
From Ulf

Dear Sis,
Having loads of fun, mainly praying to ~~god~~ **God** for the icicles in my sleeping bag to melt. You were sure right about camping being cool. Saw ~~venus~~ **Venus** last night through a hole in the tent, although Wozza thinks it was a piece of HMD's dandruff. Anyway, I think we should get a caravan next year (but it has to be a ~~ferrari~~ **Ferrari**).
S-s-s-see you, F-F-F-Flash

Use capital letters for **days**, **months**, **religious festivals**, **planets** and more:
Monday **A**pril **R**amadan **P**luto **H**oly **B**ible

7 Speak up!

Capital letters: Use for beginning speech

It's midnight on the campsite and there are strange noises outside. Everyone creeps into Ulf's mega tent for safety. It's too dark to show you what terrible things are happening, so here's the story …

The frightened children huddle together in Ulf's tent. Suddenly, there's a loud scream outside.

'Arrrreeuuurggghhhoouucchh!'

Wozza gulps and whispers, '**W**hat's *that*?'

Max replies, '**I**t sounded like a screech to me.'

HMD says, '**N**o, it was more like a wail.'

'**W**ell, this *is* wails', says Ulf.

Googal replies, '**D**on't start *that* again. Anyway, it was definitely a groan.'

There's silence for a few seconds, then the sound of heavy footsteps …

Flash says, '**W**ait, I can hear the sound of heavy footsteps.'

'**O**nly one person has footsteps that heavy,' says Deej.

'**M**R SUMO!' they all shout.

'**M**r Sumo, is that you outside?' says Max.

'**E**r, no,' says Mr Sumo. 'It's someone else.'

HMD said, '**W**ell, who screeched?'

Mr Sumo answers, '**I** stubbed my toe on a tent peg. And it was a yell, anyway.'

Ulf says, '**D**on't worry about your toe – we're sending out Shagpile to bite it better.'

And, strangely enough, as they peer out into the night, Mr Sumo's nowhere to be seen.

Cheesy Chad says …

Look – when each person starts to speak, there's a capital.

8 Poetry please!

Capital letters: Beginning a line of poetry

Googal has suggested that the gang write some poems to help them remember their holiday. Only Max and Deej manage one.

Come on, Max and Deej – read your poems out.
Oh everyone here loves to camp,
Though it's freezing, uncomfy and damp.
But looking back we'll be glad
Of experiences had –
Mainly bruises and coughing and cramp.
Dad lent
Me a tent,
Got bent
In Gwent,
Money spent,
Letter sent,
Big lament,
I repent.
Remember that each line of a poem begins with a capital letter.

Don't worry – we promise they won't write any more.

9 A quick recall

Holiday's over – time to go home.

Did you enjoy the scenery in Wales, Ulf?
I didn't see any – there were all these mountains in the way.

Use a Capital Letter

To begin every sentence.
When someone speaks, 'OK?'
For people's names.
For titles of books, films etc.
For names of organisations.
For names of places.
For beginning lines of poems.
For the word I.
Don't forget days and months.

For some reason, they've decided not to go camping next year.

Multiple Joyce

Which of these is correct?

A Mr Sumo
B mr sumo
C mR sUMO
D Missed 'er mum.

Full Stops

The Circus

Full stops:
Mark the end of a sentence

1 The circus is coming to town

The Odd Mob have found a puzzling poster on a wall. It doesn't make a lot of sense as all the full stops are in the wrong places.

Biffo's Circus.
Is coming to town.
You'll be sorry. If you
miss it see the clowns'.
Trousers fall down.
Gasp. At the acrobats.
And the jugglers it will
be lots of fun!

It says I'll be sorry the circus is coming to town. Why's that?

Because if you miss it you have to see the clowns.

No, it's because it'll make your trousers fall down and that's enough to make anyone gasp.

Remember, full stops go at the end of sentences.

If you put a full stop in the wrong place then the last part of the sentence won't make sense:

Shagpile barked. At the clowns.

② Animal rights

The Odd Mob aren't sure whether they should go to the circus.

Full stops:
Go at the end of a complete statement

I hope the circus has got elephants and tigers.

I don't like circuses if they have performing animals.

Yes, it's wrong to make animals do tricks

Oh, I don't know. I'm happy to do tricks for treats.

What happened to the boy who ran away with the circus?

The police made him give it back.

Always put a full stop at the end of a complete statement:

Googal is relieved to learn that the circus doesn't use animals to perform tricks. ✓

③ Keeping it brief

The gang are trying to save time by using abbreviations when they talk.

Full stops: Use with abbreviations

Hey, I've heard this circus is the No.1 outfit.

OK, give me an e.g. of why that is.

It's got jugglers, clowns, acrobats etc. etc.

I think you'll find that's more than one e.g.

Oh, stop showing off your I.Q., Googal.

Leave her alone, Flash. Googal is our V.I.P.

This lot go O.T.T. at times.

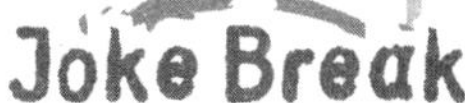

Q. How can you keep a twit busy all day?

A. Give them a piece of paper with PTO written on both sides.

Not all abbreviated words use full stops, e.g. **PTO**, **DIY**, **RAF**. Can you guess what these abbreviations stand for?

You can use full stops when you abbreviate words:
Rick O'Shay, **a.k.a.** the human cannonball, will be fired from a gun at 3 **p.m.** today.

4 The circus parade

The Odd Mob are excited to see the circus parade passing by.

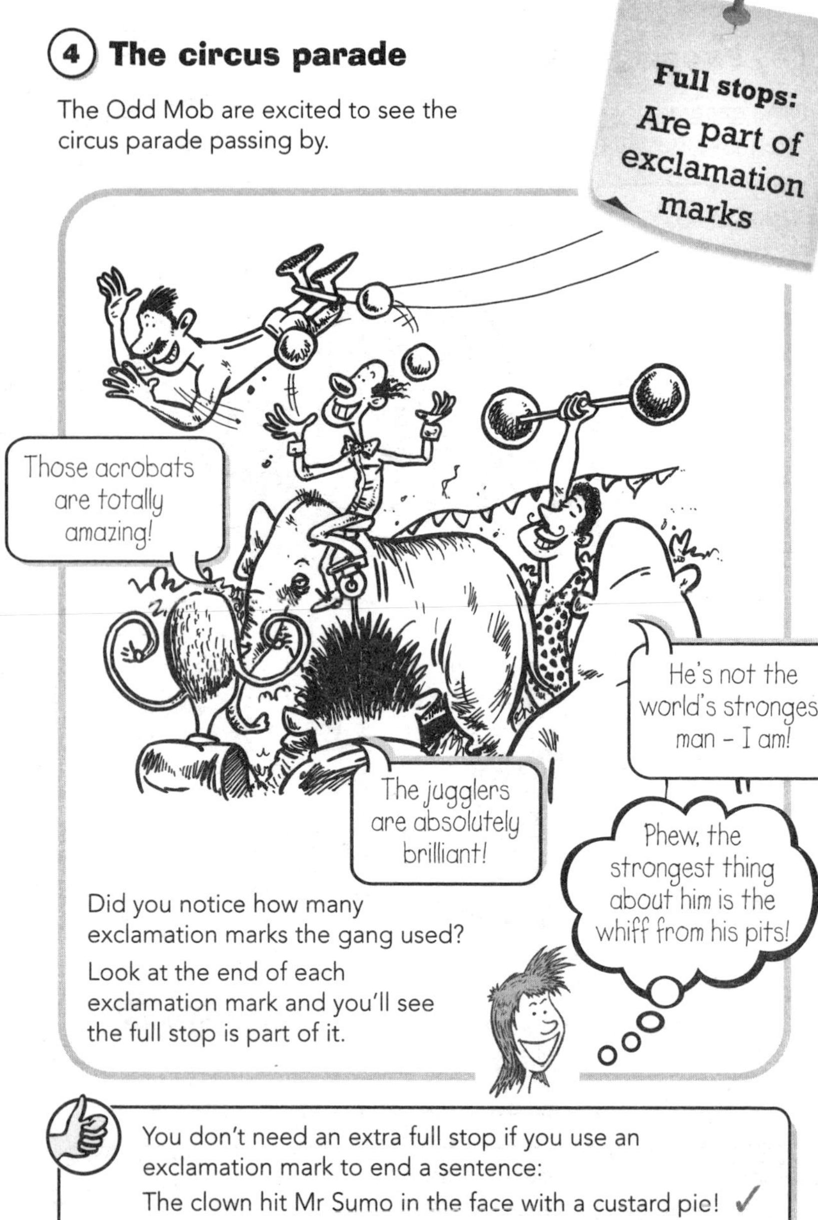

Full stops:
Are part of exclamation marks
Those acrobats are totally amazing!
The jugglers are absolutely brilliant!
He's not the world's strongest man – I am!
Phew, the strongest thing about him is the whiff from his pits!

Did you notice how many exclamation marks the gang used?

Look at the end of each exclamation mark and you'll see the full stop is part of it.

You don't need an extra full stop if you use an exclamation mark to end a sentence:

The clown hit Mr Sumo in the face with a custard pie! ✓

The clown hit Mr Sumo in the face with a custard pie!. ✗

5 The box office

The Odd Mob are trying to buy tickets for the show.

Full stops: Are part of question marks

Do you have any tickets left over for the show tonight?

Yes, lots.

So why did you print so many?

Look, do you want to buy some tickets or not?
We do, but what time does the show start tonight?
What time can you get here?

Look carefully at the question marks. Can you spot the full stops?

Questions end with a question mark – not with an extra full stop, e.g.

Why aren't clowns funny? ✓

Why aren't clowns funny?. ✗

Joke Break

Q. Why can't a clown's nose be 12 inches long?

A. Because then it would be a foot.

6 Shakespeare it isn't

Deej stumbles across a mysterious manuscript outside Bozo the clown's caravan.

Full stops: Go inside speech marks

Hey, look what I've found. It's Bozo the clown's script.
Let's see. I bet that'll be really funny.
I bet it isn't. I've seen these clowns.
Bozo says, "Everyone knows why the clown crossed the road."
Dippy says, "No they don't. So tell us why the clown crossed the road."
Bozo replies, "It was to find his rubber chicken."
I don't know what kind of eggs rubber chickens lay but the yolk's on us. We've paid for tickets to listen to this stuff.
Doh!

Joke Break

Q. Why did the clown wear loud socks?

A. To stop his feet going to sleep.

When someone is speaking, put the full stop before the last set of speech marks:

Googal said, "Even I know better jokes than that."

7 The big top

The Odd Mob take their seats in the big top.

Full stops:
Aren't needed after titles

Don't tell the **AA** but **Dr** Chuckles and his Incredible Exploding Car, **Ms** TNT, have driven all the way across the **UK** to be here tonight.
Hey, I saw them on the **BBC** the other night.
Hmm. A cop from the **CID** should arrest that clown for attempting to murder a joke.

Don't put full stops after titles or headings:

Mr Sumo **Mrs** Chuckles **CNN**
The Fantastic Flea Circus

8 The challenge

Mr Sumo challenges the circus strongman to a trial of strength.

Full stops: Go outside brackets
He looks tough (but then so does my gran's roast beef).
Huh. I've seen stronger kittens than Mr Sumo (even though they were wearing pink bows).
Cheesy Chad says ...
The full stop is the strongest punctuation mark.

Full stops should go outside, not inside, brackets:

Mr Sumo was a pussy cat (even though he thought he was a tiger).

9 A quick recall

The Odd Mob offer some useful advice.

Multiple Joyce

Which of these is correct?

A I want a. Dog
B I. Want a dog
C I want. A dog
D The dog didn't want me.

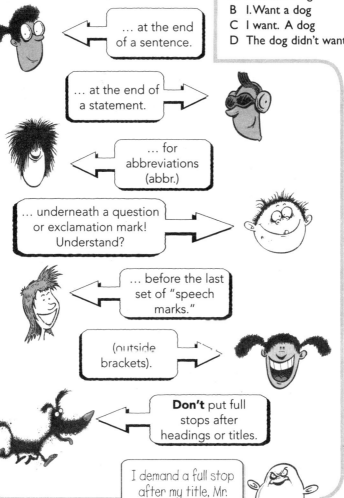

Use a full stop ...

... at the end of a sentence.

... at the end of a statement.

... for abbreviations (abbr.)

... underneath a question or exclamation mark! Understand?

... before the last set of "speech marks."

(outside brackets).

Don't put full stops after headings or titles.

I demand a full stop after my title, Mr.

Question Marks

Question Marks:
Go at the end of direct questions

1 A big question

The Odd Mob have just been watching a film about space aliens.

Do you believe in UFOs, Googal?

Not really. Do you?

Forget UFOs. Why is Shagpile barking so loudly? I can't hear myself think.

Hmm ... there are more questions than answers here. But will the Odd Mob soon be in for a surprise?

What are you trying to tell us, girl?

Has someone faller down a disused mineshaft?

Oh no! Is it me?

Don't be daft. You're here with us - aren't you?

Oh dear, do you think they're asking the wrong questions?

End every direct question with a **question mark**:
Now do you understand what to do?

2 First contact

The space alien meets the Odd Mob. They have lots of direct questions to ask.

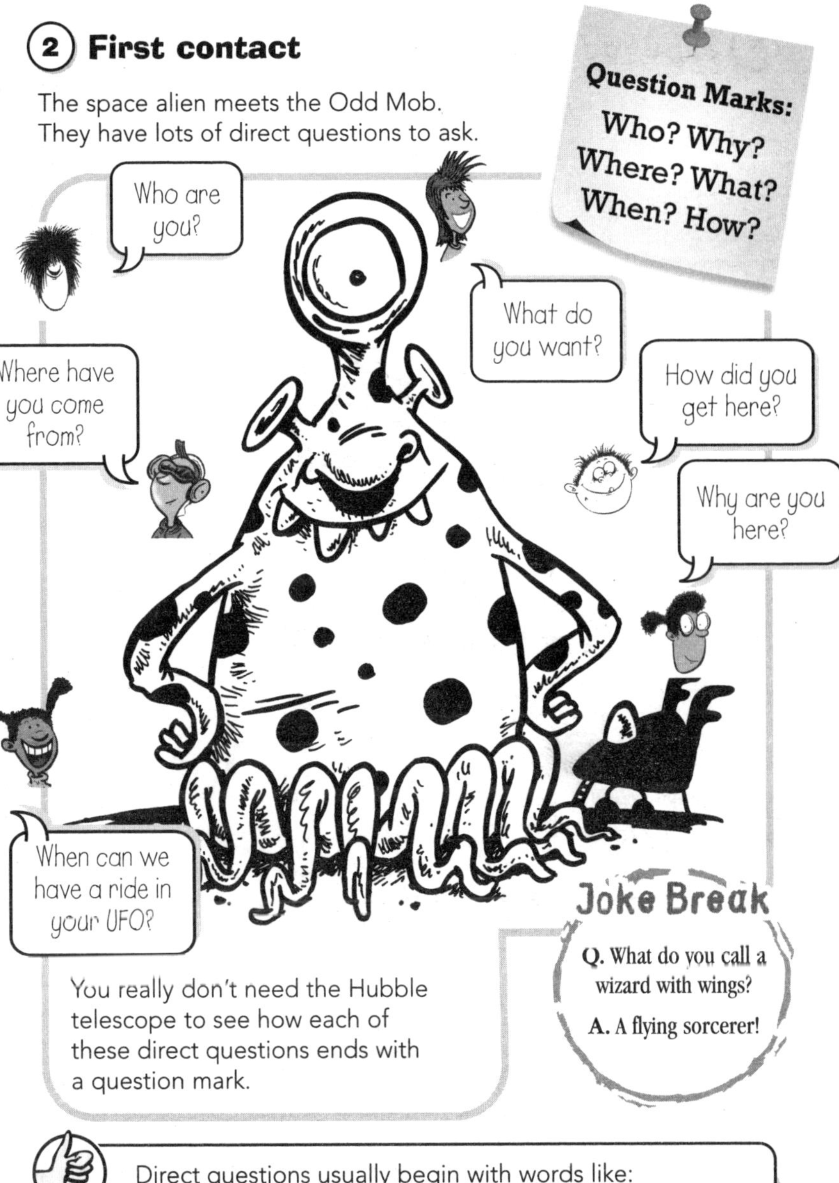

You really don't need the Hubble telescope to see how each of these direct questions ends with a question mark.

Joke Break

Q. What do you call a wizard with wings?

A. A flying sorcerer!

Direct questions usually begin with words like:
Who? What? Where? When? Why? How? Are? Is? Can? Will?

Question Marks: Indirect questions don't have question marks

3 Take me to your leader

The space alien is looking for intelligent life.

Can you take me to your leader?

Hey, the alien asked if we could take it to our leader.

Look, no question mark.

Do any of you understand me?

Wow! It's asking if any of us understand it.

Look, no question mark.

Who is in charge here?

Crikey. It wants to know who is in charge here.

Woof! Woof!

Look, no question mark.

Did you notice how when the Odd Mob repeated the alien's questions (**indirect questions**) they didn't have a question mark?

In an **indirect question**, where the speaker's exact words aren't repeated, you **don't** need a question mark:

The alien asked if dogs were the most intelligent life form on the planet.

4 Happy landings

Wozza wants the alien to help her solve a mystery.

Question Marks: Inside a bracket

Hey, Mr Alien, I've got a book about aliens. Take a look.
The Roswell Mystery
An alien (?) crash landed a UFO (?) in Roswell in the USA in 1947.
They put those question marks in the book because they're not sure if there really was an alien or a UFO.
Actually, it was my uncle Zupknucklez. He always was a terrible driver.

Joke Break

Q. Did you hear the joke about the UFO?

A. It was out of this world!

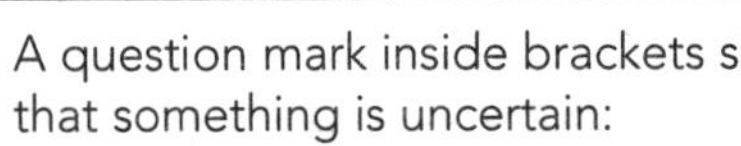

A question mark inside brackets shows that something is uncertain:

The alien's name was Zagirz (**?**) which apparently was a common name on its planet.

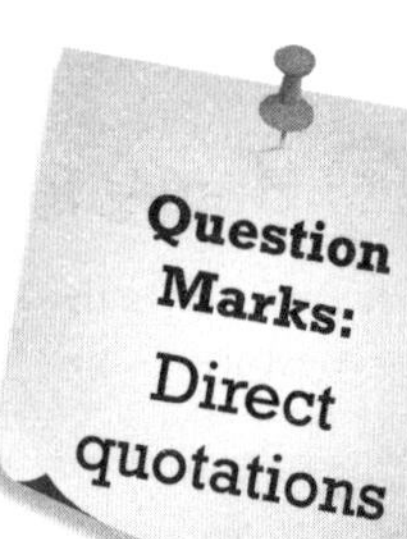

5 Hold the front page

Shagpile's a smart dog but the space alien soon realises that Googal is the brains behind the Odd Mob. Googal takes him to the town hall to meet the mayor and then the story hits the headlines.

Local Girl Meets Alien

An amazing event took place today when local girl Googal of the Odd Mob met an alien from the planet Zarg.

"Who are you**?**" she asked him.

"Why are you here**?**" she said.

"What the heck do you think you're doing**?**" she demanded as the alien tried to vaporise Mr Sumo with its ray gun.

"The alien thought I was a people-eating pink jelly," said the shaken Sumo. "It's supposed to be intelligent, so how could it have made such a mistake**?**"

Always use a **question mark** if the question is a direct quotation that repeats the speaker's exact words:

"How could anyone mistake me for a giant jelly?" asked Mr Sumo.

6 A quick recall

Meeting the alien was really exciting, so the Odd Mob are making a scrapbook about their adventure. Let's have a look at it.

A direct question always ends with a question mark.

The alien asked us if Shagpile's name was Woof.

An indirect question **doesn't** have a question mark.

The alien spoke a language called Xanpitinz (?) that sounded really weird.

Use a question mark **inside** a bracket if you're not sure about a fact.

"What are you doing with that ray gun?" spluttered Mr Sumo.

You always use a **question mark** if the **question** is a **direct quotation**.

Oh dear, the Men in Black have told the Odd Mob they can't tell anyone about the alien, so we'd better stop now before they get into trouble.

Exclamation Marks

A Visit to the Chocolate Factory!

The exclamation mark:
Use for an outburst

1 Choc full of exclamations!

The gang visit the local choccy factory. Fancy letting them in!

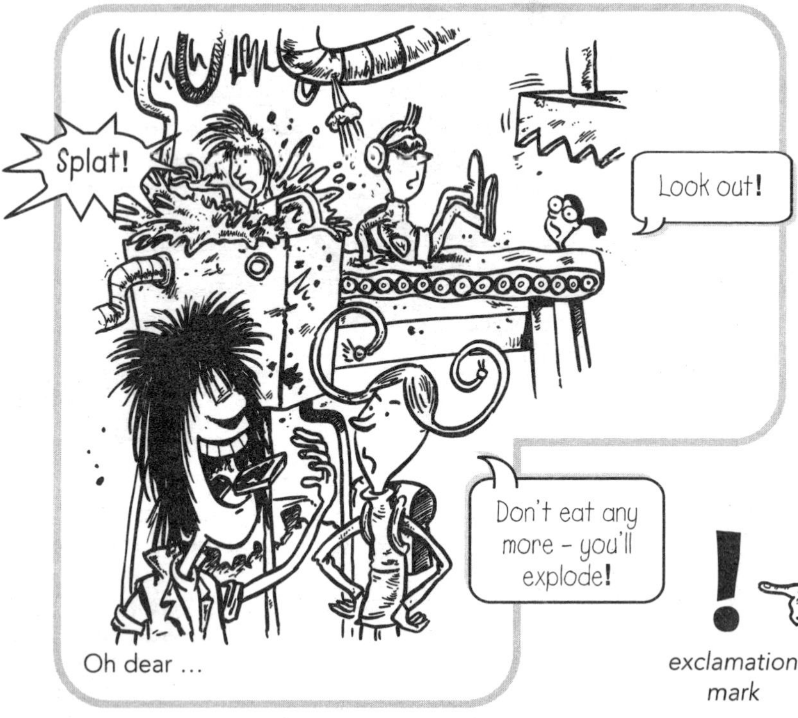

Splat!

Look out!

Don't eat any more – you'll explode!

Oh dear …

!

exclamation mark

Exclamation marks are used for:
a surprise (Wow!) or **an outburst** (Quick! Run!)

2 Mad management

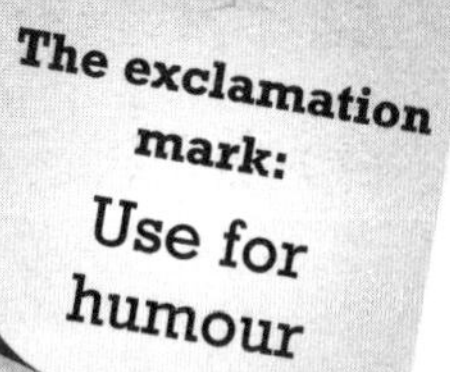

The gang are rounded up and taken to the manager's office.

Oh, thank you very much, children! That *was* helpful!

Some of the gang are confused – it doesn't *seem* like they've been helpful. Then Googal explains to them that the manager is being **sarcastic**.

Exclamation marks can be used to show **sarcasm** in a piece of writing. It's a type of humour (but not really funny, is it?). The gang prefer slapstick themselves.

Cheesy Chad says ...

Exclamation marks can show **humour**:
The visit to the chocolate factory was *not* a huge success!

The exclamation mark:

Don't overuse it

③ Oops – sorry!

The next day, Flash decides to write a letter to the manager of the factory to apologise for the mess.

Dear Mr Manager!
We enjoyed visiting your factory very much! The gang and I are sorry that we ate and spoiled so much choc! We won't do it again – well, not for a while, anyway!!!
Love from Flash!

Googal checks the letter, as usual. She says just one thing. Too many exclamation marks, especially at the end! So Flash changes the letter:

Dear Mr Manager,
We enjoyed visiting your factory very much. The gang and I are sorry that we ate and spoiled so much choc. We won't do it again!
Regards, Flash

That's better. The manager is pleased to get the letter (although he's banned the gang anyway …).

Try not to use too many exclamation marks: Only use **one** at a time!! (oops)

4 A quick recall

There were a lot of exclamations when the gang visited the choccy factory. Let's think back …

Exclamation marks are used for:

1. Surprise or astonishment:

Max has fallen in!

2. An outburst:

Yikes!

3. Humour, such as sarcasm:

I *love* having kids in the factory!

Joke Break

Q. Why do birds fly south in winter?

A. It's too far to walk!

Multiple Joyce

Which of these is a common exclamation?

A etc!
B 35 1/2!
C Ouch!
D Halibut!

Remember:

Use them only when you need to and only use one at a time.

Commas

The Shopping Expedition

Commas:
Separate the items in a list

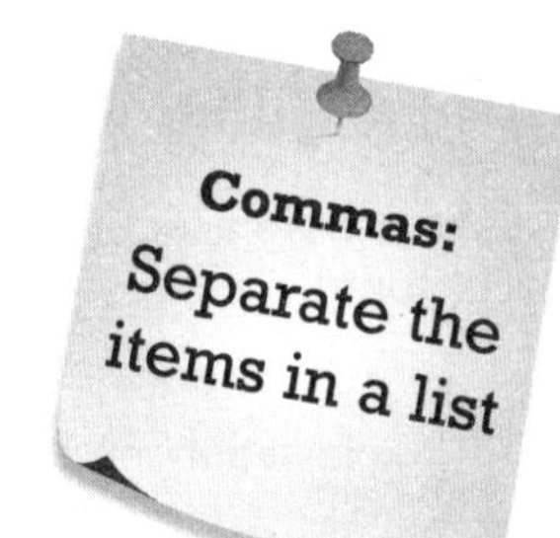

1 Making a list

The Odd Mob decide that they need to cheer themselves up. Deej suggests that they go shopping. They all agree but Googal says they must make a list of what it is they want to buy before they go.

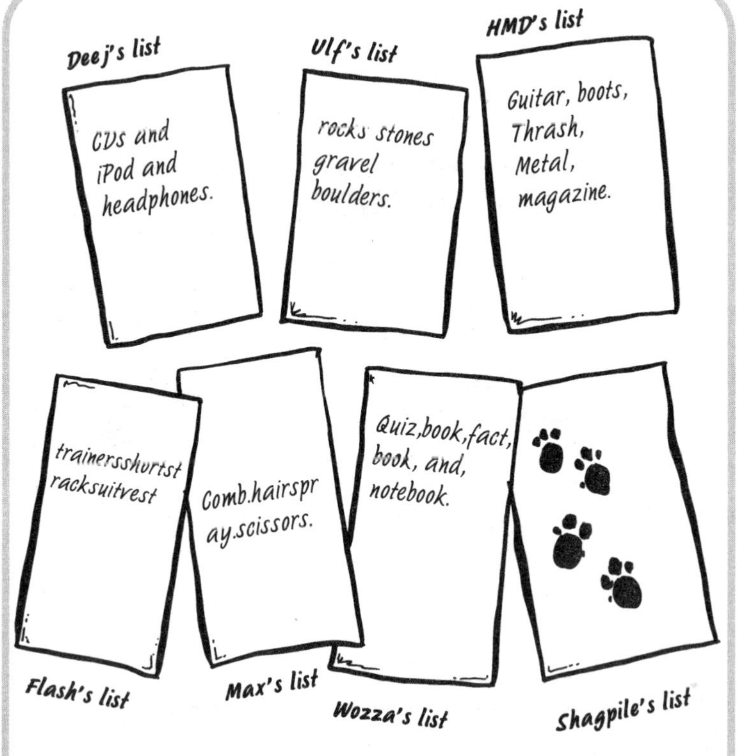

Deej's list
CDs and
iPod and
headphones.
Ulf's list
rocks stones
gravel
boulders.
HMD's list
Guitar, boots,
Thrash,
Metal,
magazine.
trainersshortst
racksuitvest
Flash's list
Comb.hairspr
ay.scissors.
Max's list
Quiz,book,fact,
book, and,
notebook.
Wozza's list
Shagpile's list

They don't look right, do they?

List of useless things:
Non-stick Sellotape, inflatable dartboards, silent alarm clocks, fireproof matches and waterproof teabags.

Googal takes one look at the lists and rewrites them using commas to separate out the items.

Deej's list
CDs, iPod and headphones.

Ulf's list
Rocks, stones, gravel and boulders.

HMD's list
Guitar, boots and Thrash Metal magazine.

Flash's list
Trainers, shorts, tracksuit and a vest.

Max's list
Comb, hairspray and scissors.

Wozza's list
Quiz book, fact book and notebook.

Shagpile's list

Did you notice that 'Thrash Metal' is the title of a magazine, so 'thrash' and 'metal' don't need to be separated from each other by a comma?

Always use commas to separate items in a list:
Googal**,** HMD**,** Deej**,** Ulf**,** Wozza**,** Max and Shagpile.

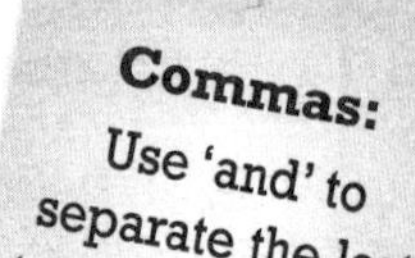

Commas:
Use 'and' to separate the last two items on a list

(2) Checking it twice

Googal has been so busy checking everyone else's list that she's nearly forgotten to write her own. But why has she written the word '**and**' instead of using a comma after the word 'skirt'?

I need some new shoes, a coat, a skirt and a top.

Hmm. I'll need to do some odd jobs to get the cash to pay for that lot. I could mow the lawn, do the washing-up, clean the house **and** then have a lie down.

Commas separate all the items on a list except the last two.

Always use the word **and** before the last word in a list:

Baked beans, eggs, sausages **and** mushrooms.

Football, cricket, tennis **and** rugby.

③ Rock on

While the rest of the Odd Mob head for the shops, Ulf goes to the quarry.

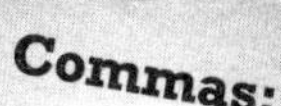

Commas:
Don't use commas when you need a full stop

So you want to buy boulders, stones and gravel. Why do you want to do that?

I'm building a rock garden. It's an Ulf thing.

Joke Break

Two's company, three's The Musketeers

Each of these four sentences makes sense on its own so they are separated by full stops, not commas.

If an idea can make sense on its own it needs to end with a full stop, not a comma:

Shagpile is a clever dog. She wants to buy her own bones.

4 An explosive situation

Ulf's dead set on buying rocks for his garden.

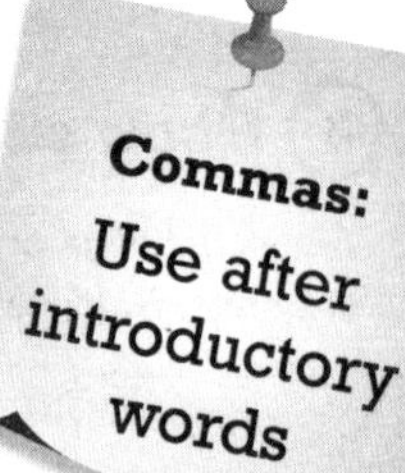
Commas:
Use after introductory words

Happily, the man at the quarry agrees to sell Ulf some large rocks.

However, they aren't big enough for Ulf.

Stupidly, Ulf decides to use dynamite to blast out some bigger ones.

Well, I'm sure he didn't mean to cause so much damage.

Always put a comma after introductory words like **yes, however, well, no**:

No, Ulf isn't really a walking disaster area – honest.

5 Shop till you drop

Deej and Max are running the poor shop assistant ragged.

Commas:
Can link short sentences with joining words

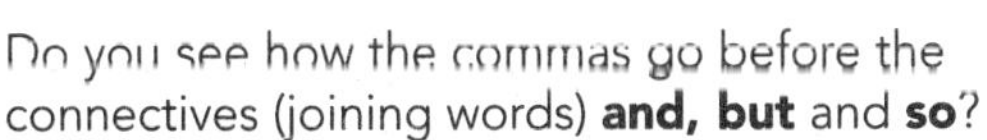

These combat trousers are old, **so** I need a new pair.
I want a designer T shirt, **and** I want a pair of designer jeans.
Max does need new combats, **but** she needs a haircut even more.

Do you see how the commas go before the connectives (joining words) **and, but** and **so**?

Joke Break

Q. What did the plain pencil say to the well-dressed pencil?

A. You look sharp!

You can use a comma before connectives like **and**, **but**, **for**, **or**, **nor**, **so** and **yet** to join two short sentences together:

Deej bought a T-shirt, **and** Max bought a pair of combat trousers.

Commas:
Can replace pronouns

(6) More haste, less speed

Wozza has taken ages to do all her shopping. Flash hasn't.

Today I went to the shops. I browsed around. I took my time. I made my selection. I bought loads of things.

So did I but I was so quick that on my way back I met myself going to the shops.

Poor old Wozza, she can't keep up with Flash. But she could speed things up by removing the 'I' from her sentences, adding some commas and turning what she has to say into a list:

Today I went to the shops**,** browsed around**,** took my time**,** made my selection and bought loads of things.

Turn short sentences into lists by taking out the noun or pronoun and **replacing them with commas**:

Flash dashed to the shops**,** (she) raced around**,** (she) grabbed some clothes and paid for them.

7 Enough is as good as a feast

HMD and Googal are taking a lunch break.

Commas: Mark the less important bits of a sentence

Actually, **although shopping's great,** I much prefer sitting here eating sausages and chips.
Your meal, **which isn't a very healthy option,** is absolutely dripping with calories.
Gosh, **chips and sausages are full of fat,** what can I do?
It's OK, **don't panic,** I can help you out.
Googal, **you're very kind,** so why do I feel I've been conned?
You know, **although I'd love to tell you,** it would be rude to speak while my mouth's full.

You can make sentences more interesting by adding extra information. **Commas** mark this extra, non vital, information.

Use commas around information that isn't essential to the meaning of the sentence:

Googal**, the smart one in the Odd Mob,** has bought some incredible clothes.

8 The power of advertising

Flash is in a sports shop when a poster of a familiar figure catches her eye.

Commas: Separate direct quotes from the rest of the sentence

"Powdered water is a great tonic, if you can find something to add to it," says wrestling champion Mr Sumo.

"Mr Sumo's as much use as a waterproof sponge, and that's the truth," says the world's fastest girl.

Commas can be used before a quotation:

Wozza said**,** "I think money spent buying books is money well spent."

⑨ A quick recall

The Odd Mob are exhausted but happy after their shopping expedition.

We must have spent a fortune. We've bought a skirt, shoes, CDs, jeans, magazines, books and a very large rock.

There are a lot of commas separating the items on this list, but then the Odd Mob bought a lot of items. This includes the very large rock that is the last item on the list, **so is joined to the list by the word 'and' instead of a comma.**

Hey, Dudes, get a load of this T-shirt.

Commas separate the introductory words from the rest of the sentence.

Commas separate two complete sentences linked together by a joining word like **and**, **but** or **so**.

I bought a book, **but** HMD bought a magazine.

Today, **although it was cold**, I went shopping.

Commas show the less important parts of a sentence.

Commas separate direct quotes from the rest of the sentence.

"I only buy designer gear," said Deej.

I think the Odd Mob will be doing odd jobs for months to try and replace all the money they've spent.

Semicolons

The Big Sleepover

Semicolons: Are stronger than commas

1 The midweek movie

Googal is having a sleepover at her house for the girls in the Odd Mob.

Googal is sorting out the entertainment for the sleepover; she's making a list of which type of DVDs the girls like to watch.

Flash likes action films;
Max likes rom-coms.
Wozza likes documentaries;
I like foreign films.

This is a piece of cake: all I have to do is find a romantic action comedy with subtitles based on a true story.

Don't forget abou
me: I like shaggy
dog stories.

In their sentences, Googal and Shagpile have both linked similar ideas together by using **semicolons**.

A semicolon looks like a comma with a dot above it. **;**

Semicolons are tough guys; they hold two parts of a sentence together. These two parts could work as separate sentences.

Semicolons help you link closely related ideas when you need a punctuation mark that's stronger than a comma: HMD likes heavy rock**;** Ulf prefers stones and gravel.

2 Too much choice

Googal pays her local DVD store a visit.

Semicolons: Go before words like 'however'

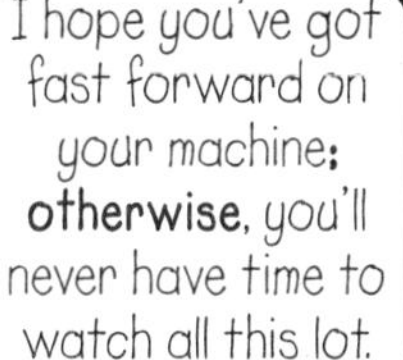

I hope you've got fast forward on your machine; **otherwise**, you'll never have time to watch all this lot.

Googal was going to choose one DVD for the sleepover; **instead**, she took the lot.

I won't watch this DVD; **indeed**, I'll wait 'til they turn it into a book.

Words like **however**, **otherwise**, **instead**, **indeed** and **therefore** are called conjunctive adverbs. They link ideas together in sentences.

Always use a semicolon before conjunctive adverbs (like **however** and **therefore**) that link two independent clauses:

Googal had a tough decision to make; **however**, Googal was up to the task.

3 Too much is as good as a feast

Semicolons: Help organise lists

The girls are setting themselves up for indigestion.

We can order a takeaway, which is cheap, quick and easy; or we can cook the food ourselves, which is hard work, time consuming and a hassle.

I vote for Chinese takeaway with spare ribs, prawn balls and rice; or pizza with chilli, tomato and cheese.

I want curry with naan bread, rice and chips; or burger, fries and cola.

Cheesy Chad says ...

Semicolons help you avoid muddling up different parts of a list.

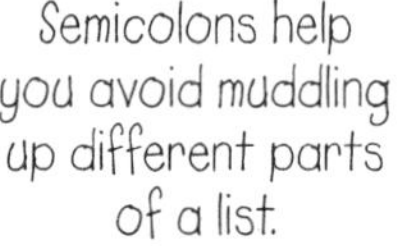

I prefer kebab with onions, cheese and chilli sauce; or tacos, refried beans and guacamole.

I think I'm going to be sick.

Use semicolons to **separate different parts of a list** if the parts already contain commas:

The girls could eat home-cooked food like lentils, beans and rice; takeaway fast food like hamburgers, hot dogs and pizza; or even a few sandwiches, cakes and pastries.

4 Rules are rules

To make sure nobody does anything silly, Wozza has drawn up some rules for the sleepover.

Semicolons: Organise lengthy clauses

Wozza's rules

During the sleepover it is not allowed to pinch other people's pillows, blankets or duvets but some people, for whatever reason, might like to swap dressing gowns, slippers and magazines this is allowed as we have all agreed this is OK.

Wozza has tried to be helpful by writing up a notice giving the rules for the sleepover. However, she's not put in any semicolons so it's a bit confusing.

Googal has rewritten the rules, putting in the missing semicolons.

During the sleepover it is not allowed to pinch other people's pillows, blankets or duvets; but some people, for whatever reason, might like to swap dressing gowns, slippers and magazines; this is allowed as we have all agreed this is OK.

Use semicolons to **separate long clauses** and avoid confusion:

The rules are quite simple**;** the girls knew what was allowed and what wasn't**;** therefore, they hoped everyone would stick to them.

Semicolons: Show contrasts

(5) No sleep till morning

Googal can't sleep at the sleepover because all the others are snoring!

Flash, Wozza and Max are fast asleep and snoring away happily**;** poor Googal can't sleep a wink.

Who started the Fire of London?
I don't know but it wasn't me.

The semicolon can be used when you want to show **contrasts** or **opposites**:

The next morning, Flash, Wozza and Max are full of beans after their nice sleep**;** Googal is a complete wreck.

6 A quick recall

Because she's so tired after the sleepover, Googal falls asleep in class the next day.

Nobody sleeps in my lessons; therefore, you're in big trouble!

Did you notice how that grumpy teacher has linked two ideas with a **semicolon** and put a comma after the conjunctive adverb? This is right, but then, she is a teacher so she should know what to do!

The teacher was cross with me; so, she's made me stay in at playtime and write an account of the sleepover; instead of waking me up this is making me fall asleep againnnn ...

You can see that Googal has used **semicolons** to separate the clauses in her account. Now the teacher's using **semicolons** in her list to separate the punishments she's planning for Googal:

Googal's Punishments
Googal could miss playtimes for a week, write lines and a letter of apology; or she could go to the head teacher, tell him what she's done and see what he has to say; or I could just send for her parents.

Multiple Joyce

Which of these is a punctuation mark?

A Semicolon
B Semi-cola
C Semicircle
D Semi-detached

Colons

Wozza's Diary!

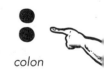

The colon:
Introduces a list

1 No picnic

Let's have a little peek into Wozza's diary for last week.

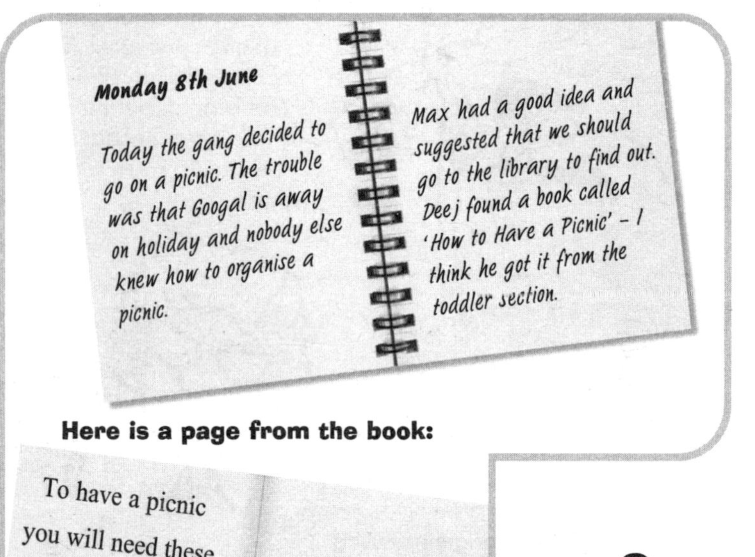

Monday 8th June

Today the gang decided to go on a picnic. The trouble was that Googal is away on holiday and nobody else knew how to organise a picnic.

Max had a good idea and suggested that we should go to the library to find out. Deej found a book called 'How to Have a Picnic' – I think he got it from the toddler section.

Here is a page from the book:

To have a picnic you will need these things: a blanket, food, drink and people.

colon

Did you notice that there is a **colon** in the book page above, after the word 'things'?

It's there to introduce a **list**.

A colon can be used to **introduce a list**:
The library had everything**:** books, tables, chairs and a roof.

2 A bit parky

The colon: Introduces speech

Here's some more of Wozza's diary …

Tuesday 9th June

Today was sunny and hot so we decided to go on our picnic. There were lots of ideas for where we should go:
HMD suggested: 'There's a Septic Mangle gig on in town – we could have it there.'
Max had a better idea: 'What about the beach?'
Ulf said: 'No way – I'm scared of sand.'
In the end, Deej solved the problem: 'Let's go to the park, then we can play Frisbee with the paper plates as well!'

Are you sure this is the right kind of basket for a picnic?
I meant with the plates, not the pies, Ulf!

There are four **colons** in Wozza's diary page above. Each one is used to introduce someone **speaking**.

A colon can be used to **introduce a speech or quotation:**

The sign in the park said: 'NO LOBBING PIES'.

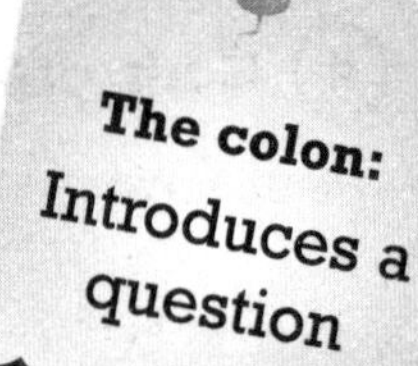
The colon:
Introduces a question

3 Flash dash

I bet you want to know what they did on Wednesday...

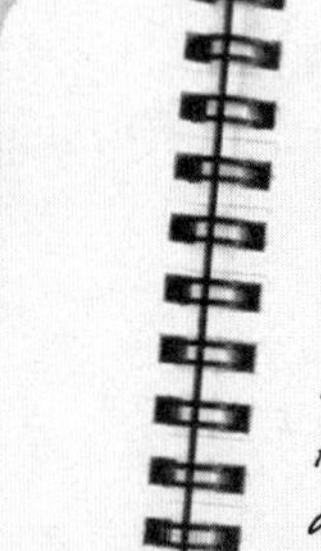

Wednesday 10th June

Today was very boring. There was nothing to do until HMD noticed something: where was Flash? She wasn't with us and she wasn't at home: where could she be? Then Max remembered seeing her looking at the karts back in the park: was she there?

Joke Break

Eric: I can jump higher than a bus.

Derek: Oh, sure...

Eric: Buses can't jump, you noodle.

Flash was at a karting race in the park ...

Flash, you won the race!

But you hate driving.

Oh, the karts were too slow anyway: I ran.

See the three **colons** in Wozza's diary page above? Look how each one comes before a **question**.

A **colon** can be used to **introduce a question:**
Flash had only one thought**:** why were the karts so slow?

4 Room for improvement

More of Wozza's diary for you!

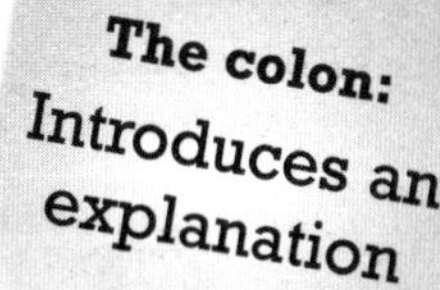
The colon:
Introduces an explanation

Thursday 11th June

Stayed at home today and tidied my room. I could tell it needed doing: I couldn't find my bed!
I thought that it was going to take me hours but it was done quite quickly. I just needed a place to put all the mess and I soon found it: my sister's room.

Cheesy Chad says ...

Notice that the word after a colon doesn't need to have a capital letter (unless it's a name).

A **colon** can be used to tell a reader that an explanation is coming up. Wozza has used two colons in her diary to help **explain** things. Can you see how they work?

A **colon** can **introduce an explanation**:

Wozza's room is tidy but there's one problem: her sister has gone ballistic ...

The colon:
Used in play scripts

5 Unfair play

What happened to Wozza and the gang on Friday? Here's some more diary for you to read:

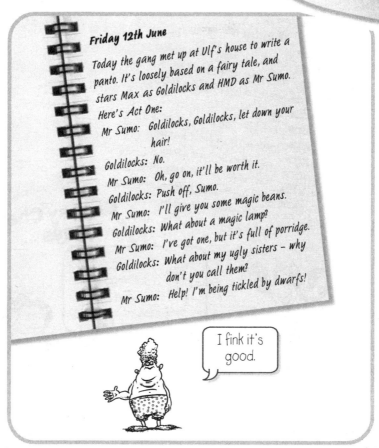

Friday 12th June

Today the gang met up at Ulf's house to write a panto. It's loosely based on a fairy tale, and stars Max as Goldilocks and HMD as Mr Sumo.

Here's Act One:

Mr Sumo: Goldilocks, Goldilocks, let down your hair!
Goldilocks: No.
Mr Sumo: Oh, go on, it'll be worth it.
Goldilocks: Push off, Sumo.
Mr Sumo: I'll give you some magic beans.
Goldilocks: What about a magic lamp?
Mr Sumo: I've got one, but it's full of porridge.
Goldilocks: What about my ugly sisters – why don't you call them?
Mr Sumo: Help! I'm being tickled by dwarfs!

I fink it's good.

Mmm … The play isn't very good, is it? But one thing is right: the gang have used colons correctly to show the lines each character has to speak.

Colons can be used to show who **speaks** in a **play script**:
Mr Sumo: Tubby or not tubby, that is the question.

6 A quick recall

The last instalment of Wozza's week:

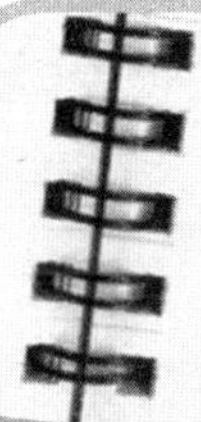

Saturday 13th June & Sunday 14th June

Spent the whole weekend sorting out my sister's room. We found all sorts of scraps of paper ...

Part of Ulf's recipe for rock soup:

To make rock soup you will need the following: 20–30 large rocks, some water and a bath.

This shows that **colons** can introduce a **list**.

A bit of Max's story about Shagpile:

Shagpile was confused: if Jo wanted the stick back, why did she keep throwing it away?

This shows that **colons** can introduce a **question**.

A scrap from the gang's pantomime:

Goldilocks: Oh no you're not daft!

Mr Sumo: Oh yes I am!

This shows that **colons** can be used in **play scripts**.

A piece of Googal's story about Elvis:

Then Elvis said: 'You ain't nothing but a hound dog, vicar.'

This shows that **colons** can introduce **speech** or a **quotation**.

A page from Deej's book about picnics:

The picnic basket was almost empty: Shagpile looked very full.

This shows that **colons** can introduce an **explanation**.

Multiple Joyce

Which of these colons is in the right place?

A Ulf: Boo!
B Ulf! Boo:
C :Ulf! Boo
D Boo: Ulf!

Thanks for the look at your diary, Wozza!

Quotation Marks

Treasure Hunt Trauma

Quotation marks:
Used for speech

1 Don't quote me

The mob are doing a treasure hunt in the park, organised by the local youth club.

Quotation marks are used to show the words that people say:

"No Ulf,**"** says Max, **"**it's not that kind of treasure hunt.**"**

Use **quotation marks** to show when someone is **speaking**:
"I've bought a cutlass just in case," says Ulf.

2 Quiz hunters

The kids have to earn clues to the location of the treasure by answering quiz questions.

Quotation marks:
Also called inverted commas or speech marks

Do we need a map and compass?
No, just a quiz sheet.
Where's the ship?

Quotation marks are sometimes called **inverted commas**. They're also called **speech marks** because they show speech:

"Where's the ship?**"** says Ulf.

Joke Break

Q. How much did the pirate's hook and peg cost him?

A. An arm and a leg.

Quotation marks, inverted commas and **speech marks** are all the same.

Quotation marks: Double or single

3 Prize problems

The gang are hoping to win something cool.

What's the prize for this treasure hunt, then?

A week in Bognor. The runner up gets two weeks.

No, it's a year's supply of turkeys to light.

You mean Turkish delight, you noodle!

Quotation marks can be **double**:

"What's the prize for this treasure hunt, then?**"** says Deej.

They can also be **single**:

HMD replies, **'**A week in Bognor ...**'**

But they should not be mixed up in one piece of writing.

Single quotation mark

Double quotation marks

Both **double** and **single** quotation marks are used to show dialogue (speech).

4 Roman around

The first question is a killer ...

Quotation marks:
Show quotations from books, people etc

Which character said, 'Lend me your ears'?
Bugs Bunny?
Pardon?
It was Julius Caesar in the play by William Shakespeare, of course.

'Lend me your ears' is a **quotation** from a play, so it's put in quotation marks.

Show a **quotation** within **dialogue** like this:

Wozza says, **"**Which character said, **'**Lend me your ears**'**?**"**
or
Wozza says, **'**Which character said, **"**Lend me your ears**"**?**'**

5 Title tattle

Quotation marks: Used for titles

Thanks to Googal, the gang begin to earn clues to win the treasure.

Who wrote the novel 'Little Women'?
Barbie?
Minnie Driver?
The book was written by Louisa May Alcott – I've read it, naturally.

Quotation marks are sometimes used to show the **titles** of books, films, TV shows, newspapers and the **names** of ships, shops, pubs, etc. within sentences.

Cheesy Chad says ...

In print, titles can also be shown in *italics* instead of quotation marks: *King Kong* is a fun film.

Titles in sentences are often written in quotation marks:

'Blue Peter' 'The BFG' 'Jurassic Park'

6 Nutmeg knowledge

Quotation marks:
Used for slang and other phrases

The Odd Mob need to answer one final question to win the treasure …

What does the expression 'to nutmeg' someone mean?

Er, it's ... er ..., I, em ... I don't know.

Simple: it's when you kick the ball through someone's legs in footy.

What! Googal didn't know something but Ulf did! Did you notice that 'to nutmeg' is in quotation marks above because it's a special football expression?

Quotation marks are sometimes used when writing slang or special words:

'Pack it in' 'hands-free' mobile Deej can 'moonwalk'

(7) A quick recall

The gang win a year's supply of Turkish delight. The trouble is, they scoff it all in a day …

Anyway, here's a summary of what quotation marks are used for:

1. To show direct speech:

   "That was a total Turkish troughing," says HMD.

2. To show a quotation:

   Flash says that she is 'about to explode'.

3. To show titles:

   The Mob buy a copy of 'The Complete Sweetie Diet Book'.

4. To write slang phrases and some specialist words:

   The gang are 'well chuffed' to win the treasure hunt.

Remember that quotation marks are also sometimes called **speech marks** and **inverted commas**.

Multiple Joyce

Which of these uses quotation marks correctly?

A We won "said Ulf".
B "We won said Ulf".
C 'We lost,' said Ulf.
D We 'Ulf' said one.

Punctuating Direct Speech

Direct speech:
Use quotation marks

Garden Fools

1 Granny's garden

Flash's granny pays a visit to Flash's house.

Flash, I'm too old and creaky to look after my garden any more.
Don't worry, Granny – Deej and I will come and help.

If we wrote this down as **direct speech** (dialogue), it would look like this:

Flash's granny says, "Flash, I'm too old and creaky to look after my garden any more."

"Don't worry, Granny – Deej and I will come and help," says Flash.

See how the speech marks only go around the words actually spoken: the **quotations**.

Speech marks (quotation marks) show **dialogue**:

"Ouch!" he says.

“oo”

quotation marks

② Another fine mess

The next weekend, Flash and Deej go round to the flats where Flash's granny lives.

Direct speech: Use commas before quotations

The garden's a right mess, so you'd better clear all of it.

OK, Granny Flash – we've brought some tools.

We need commas to separate the speech from the rest of the sentence:

Granny said**,** "The garden's a right mess, so you'd better clear all of it."

"OK, Granny Flash – we've brought some tools**,**" says Deej.

Cheesy Chad says ...

Sometimes, 'single speech marks' are used instead of "double ones".

Commas are used before or after a quotation:
Deej says**,** "Hello." "How do**,**" says Granny.

③ Clear as mud

Flash and Deej have a look round the garden before getting to work.

Direct speech:
Capitals start quotations

This garden's not exactly a mess.

Yeah, but she said to clear it all.

Joke Break

Kev: What's green, lives in a garden and has 8,000 legs?

Bev: Dunno.

Kev: Grass – I lied about the legs.

A **capital letter** is needed at the **start** of a quotation:

"**T**his garden's not exactly a mess," says Deej.

Flash replies, "**Y**eah, but she said to clear it all."

The words a person says always begin with a **capital letter**.
Flash says, "**G**et digging." "**O**K, OK," sighs Deej.

④ For the chop

Direct speech: Final punctuation

After a few hours working in the garden, the kids are fading.

Can we stop now? I'm exhausted!

So am I, but I want to cut down this tree.

Question marks go **inside** speech marks if the speaker asks a question:

Deej says, "Can we stop now?"

So do exclamation marks and full stops:

Deej moans, "I'm exhausted**!**"

Flash says, "So am I, but I want to cut down this tree**.**"

If a quotation ends a sentence, put the final punctuation mark before the closing speech marks:

Deej called out, "Timber!"

5 Dig this, man

Direct speech: Interrupting dialogue

Following a break, Deej and Flash continue to clear Granny's garden.

A quotation is sometimes interrupted, especially if it's two sentences.

Notice where the full stop, comma, capitals and speech marks go here:

"Help me pull up these bushes, Flash**,"** **s**ays Deej. **"T**hey're really tough."

Below, a quotation is interrupted in the **middle** of a sentence, so two **commas** are used.

"OK**,"** **s**ays Flash**,** **"w**hen I've finished digging up the lawn."

Commas and full stops are used to interrupt a quotation:
"Gardening is too slow for me," said Flash. "I can't sprint in wellies."

6 Weeding and writing

The garden work is nearly finished ...

Direct speech: Use a new line for each speaker

Nice flowers.
Yeah, it seems a shame to pull them up.
And to break up that nice patio we just smashed.

When writing dialogue, you need to start a **new line** for each new speaker:

"Nice flowers," said Flash.

"Yeah, it seems a shame to pull them up," said Deej.

"And to break up that nice patio we just smashed," said Flash.

Quotations are usually **indented**:

The children have finished digging.

← gap → "Done it," said Flash.

7 We're finished

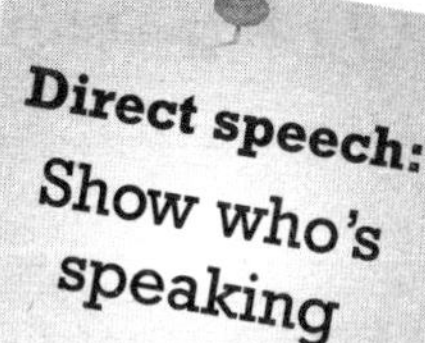
Direct speech:
Show who's speaking

They've finished! Flash and Deej call Granny over to show her their work.

There, we've cleared the lot!

What do you think?

Excellent work, kids. But my garden is that one, next door.

Oh dear … Here's the dialogue.

Flash announced, "There, we've cleared the lot!"

"What do you think?" **said Deej**.

"Excellent work, kids. But my garden is that one, next door," **replied Flash's granny**.

When several people are talking, make sure you show who said what:

"Let's scarper!" **said Flash**.

8 A quick recall

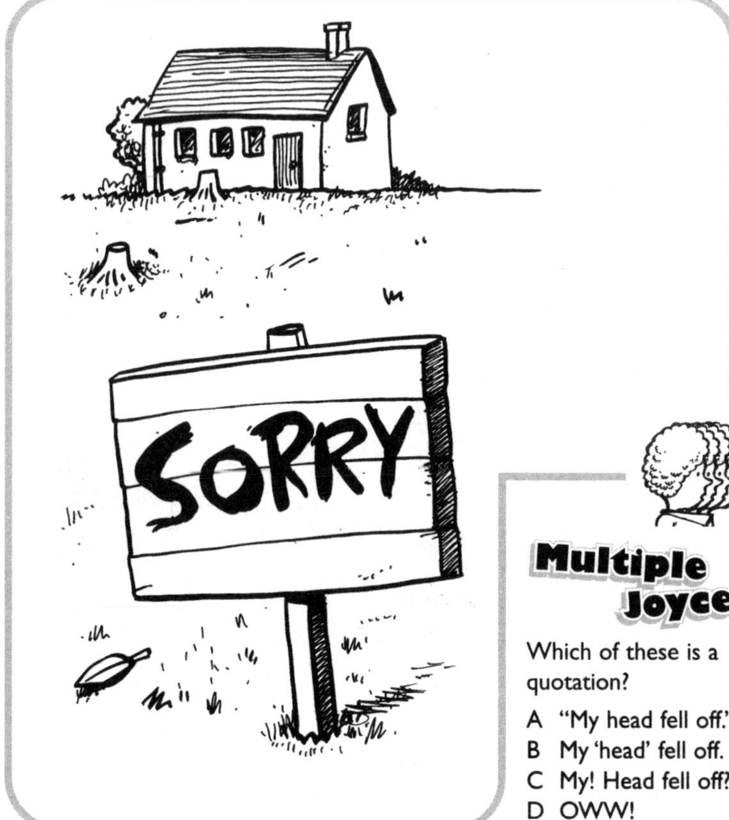

Multiple Joyce

Which of these is a quotation?

A "My head fell off."
B My 'head' fell off.
C My! Head fell off?
D OWW!

- Put **quotation marks** (speech marks) around the words people say.
- Use **commas** to introduce a quotation.
- Use a **capital letter** to start a quotation.
- Final punctuation goes **inside the speech marks** if a quotation ends a sentence.
- A quotation can be **interrupted with a comma** at the end of the first part.
- Start a **new line** for each speaker.

And don't dig up the wrong garden …

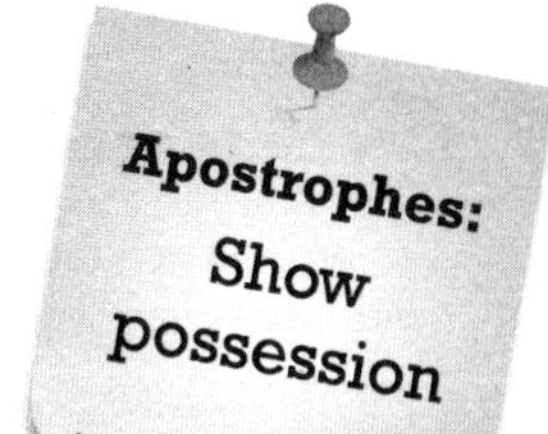

Apostrophes
Apostrophe Hospital

1 Down at the doctor's

Deej has gone to the casualty department for abused and misused apostrophes to get the label on his headphones fixed.

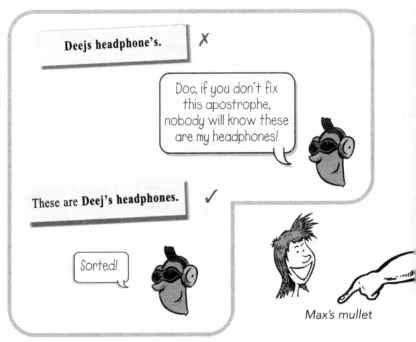

Deejs headphone's. ✗

Doc, if you don't fix this apostrophe, nobody will know these are my headphones!

These are **Deej's headphones.** ✓

Sorted!

Max's mullet

Possession means when something belongs to someone.

Apostrophes can show that something belongs to someone:

Deej**'s** headphones: the headphones belong to Deej.

Ulf**'s** head: the head belongs to Ulf (well, no one else would want it ...)

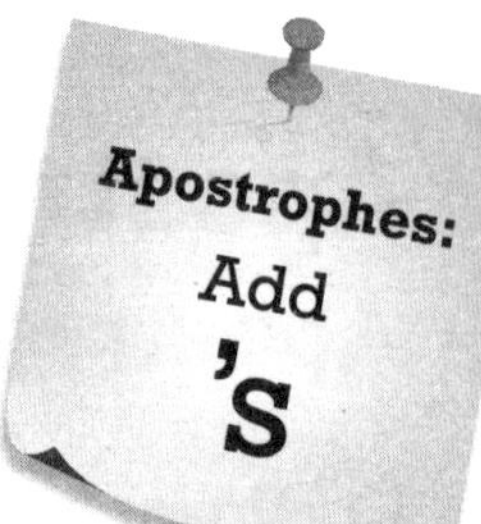

② Emergency!

An ambulance races up to the hospital with lights flashing.

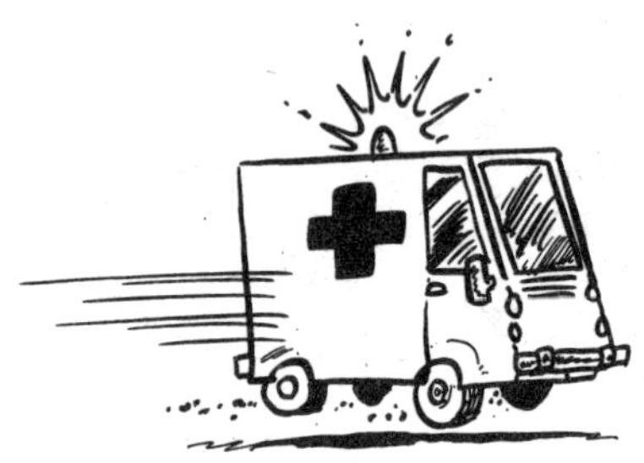

The **ambulance's** siren is wailing. This must be a real emergency.

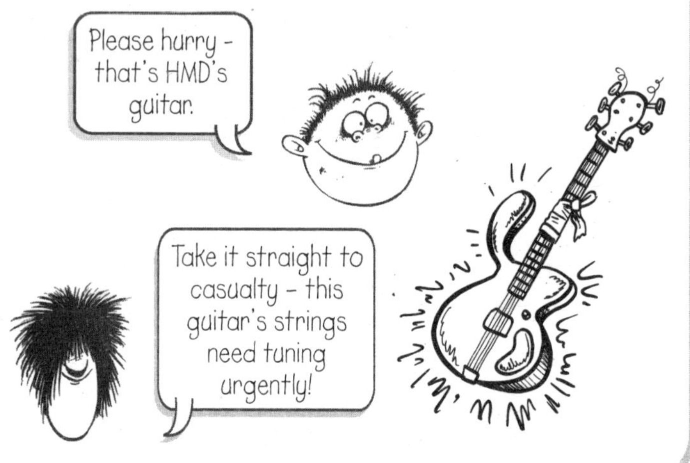

Please hurry - that's HMD's guitar.
Take it straight to casualty – this guitar's strings need tuning urgently!

If a noun (name) is singular you can show what belongs to it by adding an **apostrophe** and the letter '**s**':

The doctor**'s** stethoscope The nurse**'s** watch
Shagpile**'s** bone

3 Bull in a china shop

The disorderly orderly.

Apostrophes: Plural nouns ending in **'S**

Mr Sumo is working as an orderly on the maternity ward. He's just dropped a bedpan and woken everyone up. Now he can't hear himself think for the **babies'** squawks and the **mothers'** grumbles!

Joke Break

Patient: My hair keeps falling out. What can you give me to keep it in?

Doctor: A shoebox

For plural nouns that end in the letter 's', just add an apostrophe – not another 's' – to show what belongs to it:

The cleaner**s'** mops
The nurse**s'** hats
the doctor**s'** coats

④ Fit to bust

Ulf and HMD have each had six cans of cola from the hospital drinks machine while they've been waiting for the doctors to fix the guitar. Now they wish they hadn't.

Apostrophes:
Add 'S to plural nouns

To the Children's Ward
To the Women's Ward
To the Men's Ward

Joke Break

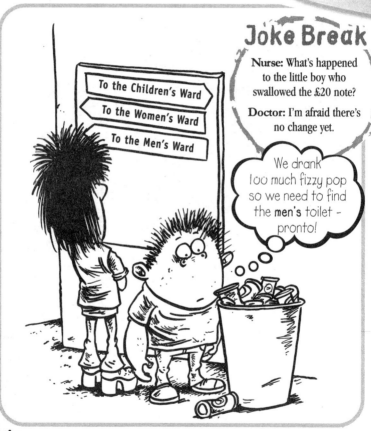

Nurse: What's happened to the little boy who swallowed the £20 note?

Doctor: I'm afraid there's no change yet.

We drank too much fizzy pop so we need to find the **men's** toilet - pronto!

If a word is plural and it doesn't end in the letter 's', you add an **apostrophe** and **s** to show possession (what belongs to it):

The **children's** toys The **people's** hospital

5 A man on omission

Flash and Shagpile are told off for running into the hospital.

Apostrophes: Show omission

There are letters missing from some of the words spoken by Flash and the nurses and thought by Shagpile. The words have been shortened and the **apostrophes** show where the missing letters should be.

Cheesy Chad says ...

Note the difference between **its** (*belonging to it*) and **it's** (*it is or it has*).

Omission means to leave something out, e.g. I'll (I **wi**ll).

Apostrophes can be used to show where missing letters from shortened words go:

I'm (I am) **You're** (You are) **She's** (She is) **It's** (It is) **They're** (They are) **We'll** (We will)

6 What's wrong here?

Send for a doctor – these apostrophes need removing.

Apostrophes: In the wrong place

WARNING NOTICE

Do not take pill 's unless given them by the doctor 's.

Oh dear. These apostrophes are wrong.

WARNING NOTICE

Do not take pills unless given them by the doctors.

That's better.

Good old Googal. She's re-written the warning notice and taken out the apostrophes from the words 'pills' and 'doctors'. They are not shortened and they do not belong to anyone – so they do not need apostrophes.

We do **not** use an apostrophe to show that there is more than one of something:

The nurse's gave Deej some injection's. ✗

The nurses gave Deej some injections. ✓

Apostrophes: Some exceptions

7 A bone of contention

The doctor is upset that someone has left an old bone in his nice clean hospital.

Shagpile dropped her bone when she was chased out of the hospital. None of the Odd Mob, except Googal, wants to accept responsibility for it. They are blaming each other.

Did you notice how possessive words like **his**, **hers**, **yours**, **its**, **ours** and **theirs** do not have apostrophes?

Joke Break

Patient: Doctor, doctor, people keep ignoring me.

Doctor: Next!

The possessive words **his**, **hers**, **theirs**, **its**, **yours** and ours are not written with an apostrophe:

"I think this bone is **yours**," said the doctor to the Odd Mob.

8 A quick recall

Deej sends a letter to the hospital and the Odd Mob receive one in return.

Dear Doc

I'm writing to say thanks for fixing my headphones. I **don't** know what I **would've** done without you.

Deej

Deej has used apostrophes to shorten words and leave out letters.

Dear Odd Mob,

Thanks for **Deej's** note. We know how he hates writing letters. We are sure his parents must be as proud of him as we would be if he were **ours**. However, will the rest of you please come and take **Shagpile's** bone home as it is starting to smell.

Doc

Oh dear, it looks like the hospital staff are not completely happy with the Odd Mob. But at least they know how to use apostrophes to show when something belongs to someone (Deej's, Shagpile's) or to a group of people (children's) – but no apostrophe if it's already a possessive word like '**ours**' or '**his**'.

Their letter also gives a useful reminder that apostrophes are not needed to show there is more than one of something, e.g. '**letters**' not '**letter's**'.

Multiple Joyce

Which of these is correct?

A apostrophe's
B a'postrophe
C apost'rophe
D a posh trophy
E apostrophes

Well, in the end the Odd Mob's visit to the apostrophe hospital hasn't been too much of a catastrophe.

Brackets

Ulf's Story

Brackets: Add information to sentences

1 Come on you wolves!

How did Ulf come to join the Odd Mob? Read on …

Ulf is an unusual boy (so some people say). According to certain members of the gang, he was brought up by wolves (although others say Everton), and lived wild in the woods until he decided to live wild in the town instead. But what is the truth? Where is he from? This section will reveal the truth (and shocking it is) … .

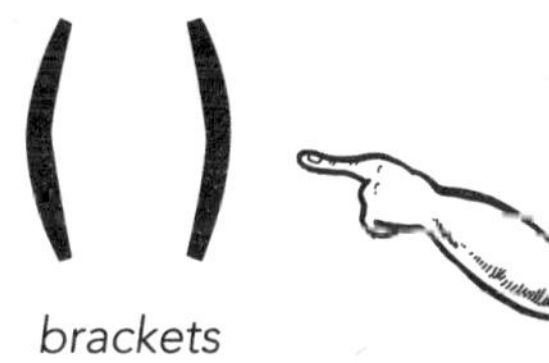

brackets

There are three pairs of **brackets** in the above paragraph (do you see how each one adds something extra to the sentence?).

Brackets can add extra **information** to writing:
Here is Ulf (a hairy boy).

2 Hair-raising stuff

Brackets: Add explanations to sentences

The story of Ulf: the beginning (see how brackets are used in it).

1. Ulf was born on Muck (a Scottish island).

2. His father (a haggis farmer) was as bald as a duck egg.

3. One day, when he was a wee toddler, Ulf found his dad's hair restorer (a product to make hair grow).

4. Ulf drank the lot!

5. A couple of days later, Ulf began to change (for the worse).

6. A month later, he looked like this (beastly!).

Brackets can add **explanations** to writing:
The island (called Muck) was small and windy.

3 Stop that rustling!

Brackets:
Can be used to make comments

So, what happened next?

1. As a boy, Ulf got a job as a shepherd (don't ask me which is him!).

BAA!
ROB CROOK & SONS

2. Then, one dark day, the sheep were stolen by some rustlers (now that's naughty). Thinking he was a grubby lamb, they took Ulf too!
3. He was never seen on the island again (poor kid).

Can you see how each phrase in **brackets** above is a **comment**?

Brackets can be used to make **comments** (what a good idea!).

4 Ransom rubbish

Brackets:
Can be used to give references

What did Ulf's parents do?

Ulf's parents went to the police, who gave them a book:

Kidnapping: 101 Tips for the Anxious Parent

Look at this page:

Kidnapping: 101 tips for the Anxious Parent

Kidnappers often ask for a ransom (see p.47). This is a sum of money which has to be paid in order for the child to be returned safely (for more information on safety, look at Appendix 5). If you pay a ransom, always ask for a receipt (see picture on p.118) and check that the child is in one piece.

12

Cheesy Chad says ...

Sometimes dashes can be used instead of brackets – see page 92.

Did you notice the three sets of **brackets** there? Each one gives a **reference** (a place to find out more).

Brackets can be used to give **references**.

5 Tree life

But we haven't found out what happened to Ulf yet!

OK, OK ...

Brackets:
Can be used to give examples

Ulf managed to escape from the robbers. For a while he lived in a tree, eating whatever he could find (e.g. apples, leaves, branches).

The tree was next to a footpath, where many people (such as ramblers) passed by. One day, Ulf slipped and fell on one of them.

It was Max!

Brackets are sometimes used to give **examples**. Notice that **commas** could be used instead of the brackets above.

Brackets can be used to give **examples** (of places, for example).

6 Rug rat

Brackets: Can be used to add detail

Here's Max to tell you the rest of Ulf's story.

Well, I remember this thing (at first I thought it was a flying rug) falling on me as I was walking along. It gave me a right shock (my heart was going like a Porsche Turbo) but then I saw two eyes and realised it was a boy (well, sort of). He said his name was Ulf and that he lived on muck. 'Well, that's no good,' I said, 'Come and join our gang and we'll give you some proper food (unless HMD is cooking). So he did and that's how Ulf joined the Odd Mob!

Joke Break

Drake: Who made King Arthur's round table?

Ann: Sir Cumference!

There.

Notice how the **brackets** above add extra **detail** to the sentences, helping the reader to understand what the writer is saying.

Brackets can add **detail** (descriptions and observations) to writing.

7 A quick recall

So that's how Ulf came to join the gang.

And this is how you can use brackets in writing:

1. To add **information:**
   Ulf lived on Muck (an island).
2. To add **comments:**
   Ulf drank hair restorer (this was wrong and stupid – don't try it!).
3. To add **explanations:**
   Poor Ulf was stolen (by heartless kidnappers).
4. To give **references:**
   The kidnap book was useless (see p.1–200).
5. To give **examples:**
   Ulf liked the Odd Mob kids (e.g. Max).
6. To add **detail:**
   Ulf joined the gang (after he realised that it was more fun than Muck).

Multiple Joyce

Which brackets are correct?

A (see p.5)
B)see p.5(
C () see p.5
D ((((((5))))))

Words in **brackets** can have their own **punctuation** (oh yes, they can!). Notice that the previous sentence still needs a **full stop** outside the brackets.

Dashes

The Cake-Baking Competition

Dashes: Stress a point

1 Googal is cooking something up

Googal thinks it would be great fun to enter a cake-baking competition. Some of the others aren't so sure.

To you lot, my idea may seem a bit crummy – or even half-baked.

What's she on about – she's nuts.

Hey, I like the idea of baking hot cakes – it's cool.

Stop dashing everywhere – I'm the runner.

Googal is keen to emphasise that her idea is very different – so she's used a dash.

HMD is just as keen to make the point that he thinks Googal's wheeze is a few currants short of a fruit slice – so he's used a dash as well.

Deej, on the other hand, wants to bake cakes, so he uses a dash to stress his support for Googal.

Flash has just missed the point.

—

A dash

Dashes can help you to make a point more strongly:

You may think I'm joking about this – you're wrong.

100-metre dash

② It's a piece of cake

Deej, Wozza and Ulf are deciding what type of cake to make.

Dashes:
Replace brackets

I'll make a chocolate fudge – **with real fudge** – cake.
I'll make a fruit – **with real fruit** – cake.

I'll make a rock – **with real rocks** – cake.

Deej, Wozza and Ulf have used dashes to separate their extra ideas from their main sentences.

Joke Break

Q. When's the best time to cook chips?

A: On a Friday.

Use **dashes** – instead of brackets – when you have an extra idea to add to your sentence:

Ulf's rock cakes should only be eaten **– and this is a serious health warning –** with your gran's false teeth.

3 Too many cooks

The gang are squabbling over who should use the oven first.

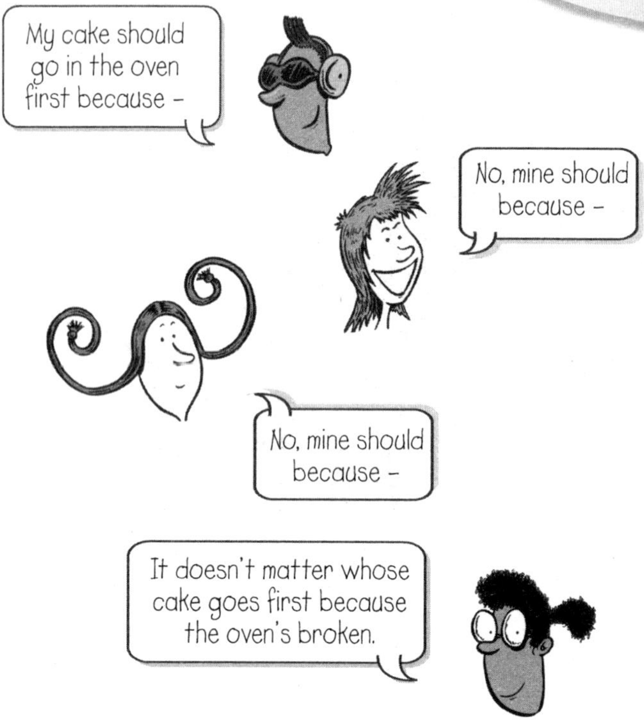

My cake should go in the oven first because –

No, mine should because –

No, mine should because –

It doesn't matter whose cake goes first because the oven's broken.

Deej, Max and Wozza each think they should be allowed to use the oven first to bake their cake. They keep interrupting each other. But Googal has the last word.

Using **dashes** to show an interruption can make the dialogue seem more urgent and exciting:

'Ulf what have you done? It looks like –' Googal gasped. Ulf had deep-fried Mr Sumo's wrestling shorts.

4 The plot thickens

Something's burning ...

Dashes: Show an abrupt change in tone

This cook book's great – but it doesn't say how to boil water.

I think my cake's ready – the smoke alarm's going off.

The **dashes** show that both HMD and Max are having second thoughts – which is surprising.

Joke Break

Customer: Waiter, what's this fly doing in my soup?

Waiter: It looks like the backstroke to me, sir.

You can use **dashes** when you want to make a sudden or surprising change in what you're saying:

Keep your kitchen spotless **–** eat out.

(5) No time to waste

Dashes:
Connect two things

A celebrity chef writes to Googal.

Dear Googal,

Thank you for entering the Cake-Baking Competition. The judging will take place at the town hall tomorrow from **1.00–2.00 pm**.

Tate Urchips

Celebrity Chef

The chef has given Googal the times when the cakes will be judged. The times are linked by a **dash** – so she'd better dash off and tell the others there's no time to waste.

The dash in '1.00-2.00 pm' replaces the word 'to' (but it has no spaces around it). A dash looks like a hyphen but it's longer.

Deej's World

What's the difference between roast beef and pea soup?

Use **dashes**, instead of the word 'to', to link two things together:

This cake recipe is suitable for children aged **3–5**.

6 It's only natural

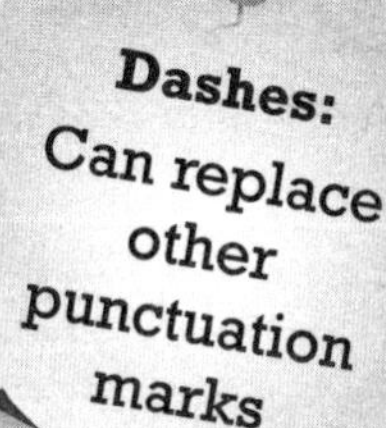
Dashes:
Can replace other punctuation marks

Ulf's rock cakes contain only organic ingredients.

The Odd Mob – Googal, Deej, HMD, Flash, Wozza, Max, and Ulf – are at the town hall for the cake judging.

The judges – Tate Urchips, Al Fresco and Dee Zaster – taste the cakes.

The information inside the **dashes** tells us who is in the Odd Mob and who the judges are.

Ulf's recipe for rock cakes – **pebbles, gravel, rocks and stones** – is a disaster for Dee Zaster. Perhaps it would have been better if she'd read the information inside the **dashes** before eating.

Dashes can replace a colon or a comma in a sentence and show more information about the subject:

All the cakes – **chocolate, fruit and sponge** – looked delicious.

7 A quick recall

Dear Ms D. Zaster

I shouldn't have used rocks in my rock cakes – **sorry**.

Ulf

Ulf's written a letter of apology to Dee Zaster and he's used a **dash** to stress how sorry he is.

Ulf – an awful cook – breaks judge's tooth with rock cake.

Ulf has hit the headlines for breaking the judge's tooth! But, instead of using brackets, the report has put the extra fact that Ulf's an awful cook as an interruption between two **dashes**.

Starter recipes:
pages 1–9

Main course recipes:
pages 10–28

Cake recipes:
pages 29–45

This page shows how Al Fresco has used **dashes** to join the page numbers together on the index page of his cookery book, 'Burnt Offerings'.

This peek at Googal's diary shows how you can use a dash to add a surprise to your writing.

Today Ulf failed his cookery exam for burning something – the school.

Hmm … Ulf's cooking is more likely to give you ache than cake.

Multiple Joyce

Which of these is a punctuation mark?

A Dash B Dasher
C Prancer D Rudolph

Hyphens
The Aquarium

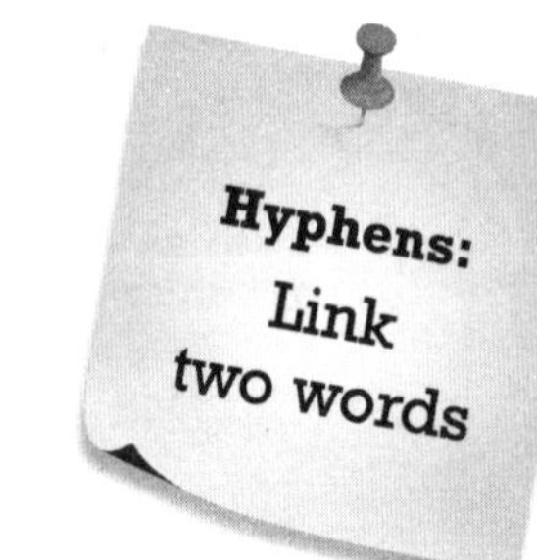

1 Making a splash

The Odd Mob have gone on a trip to the aquarium.

Are there any whales in this aquarium?

No, whales aren't fish. They're **warm-blooded** mammals.

Warm-blooded is hyphenated.

Is that so it can breathe underwater?

This is a low-budget cartoon. But we could still afford a hyphen.

Hyphens join two words together to make one new word:
Fish are **cold-blooded** creatures.

(2) Jaws

HMD and Ulf have a bit of a misunderstanding.

Hyphens: Make meaning clear

Joke Break

Ray: What do you get if you cross a great white shark with a cow?

Faye: I dunno, but I wouldn't want to mik it!

I'd rather use a harpoon if a shark attacked me.

Did you know that there are four hundred-odd types of shark?

Why are there so many odd sharks?

The sharks aren't odd. HMD means that there are about four hundred different types of shark. He used a **hyphen**.

Using hyphens can change what you mean to say:

A **man-eating** shark (a shark that eats people).

A man eating shark (is a man who is having a meal of shark and, maybe, chips).

(3) Sea spiders

Googal's knowledge of crabs is put to the test.

Hyphens:
Make adjectives from two or more words

Googal, can you tell me why these crabs are called 'spider crabs'?

It's because they're so **spider-like**.

That's a **first-class** answer, Googal.

Oh, she's a **clever-looking** girl, but she can be a bit crabby herself at times.

That's hardly surprising with **know-it-all** Deej around.

You can make new adjectives from two or more words by adding hyphens:

Googal was a girl who **looked clever**.

Googal was a **clever-looking** girl.

4 Don't break the rules

Deej and Max can be rebels sometimes.

Hyphens:
Make some words easier to read

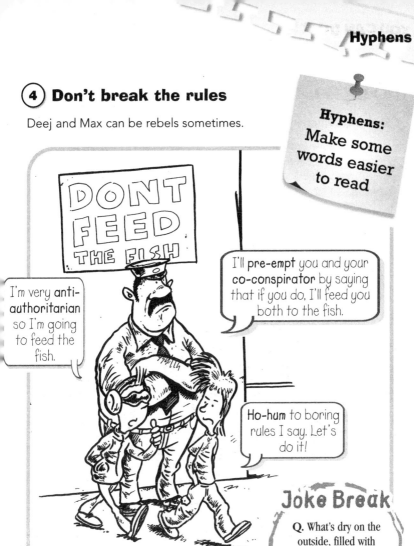

DONT FEED THE FISH
I'm very **anti-authoritarian** so I'm going to feed the fish.
I'll **pre-empt** you and your **co-conspirator** by saying that if you do, I'll feed you both to the fish.
Ho-hum to boring rules I say. Let's do it!

I think Deej and Max had better **co-operate** with the attendant.

Joke Break

Q. What's dry on the outside, filled with water and blows up buildings?

A: A fish tank!

Hyphens can separate long words, or words with identical letters next to each other, to make them easier to read:

The attendant had a word in Deej's **shell-like** ear.

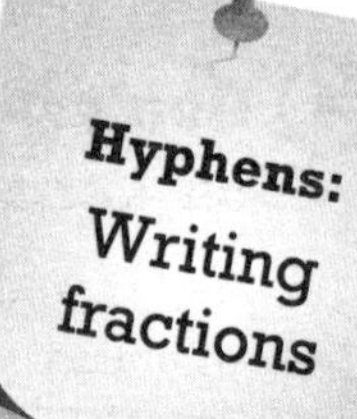

5 Ulf is half-right

You learn something new every day.

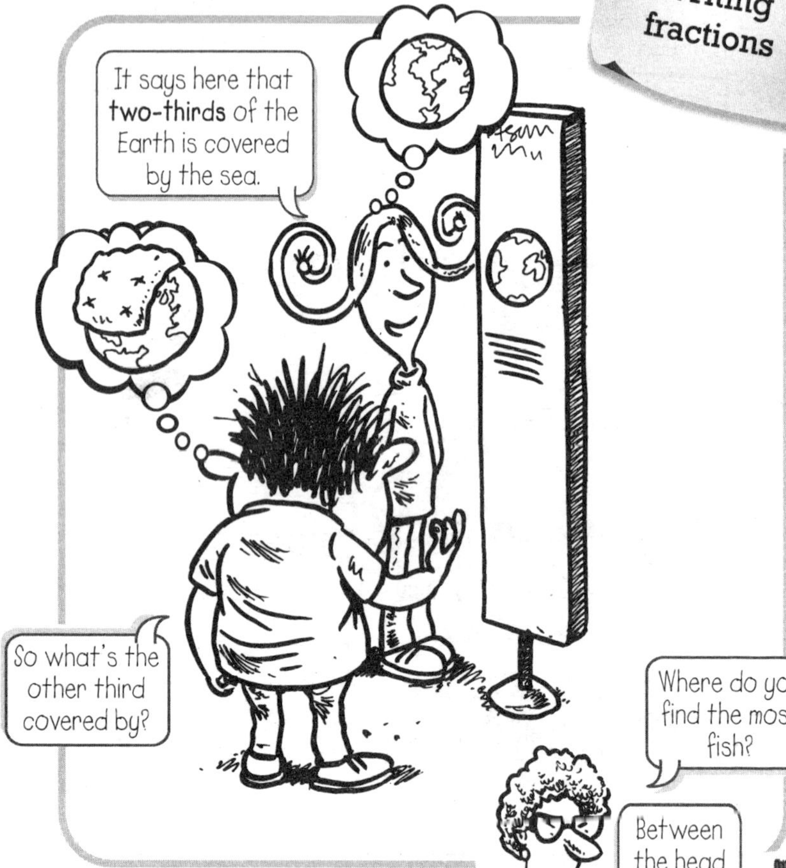

It says here that **two-thirds** of the Earth is covered by the sea.

So what's the other third covered by?

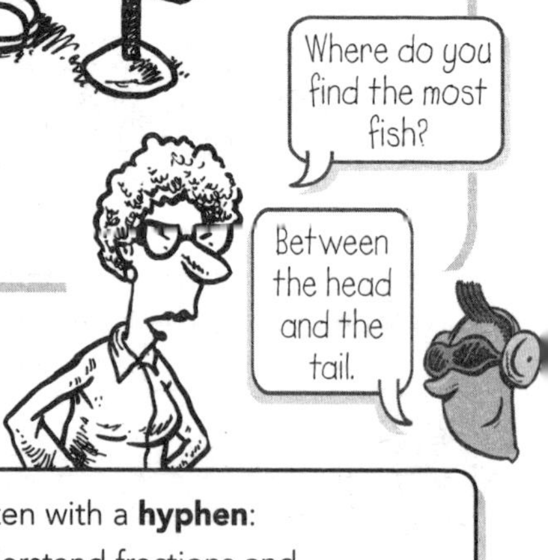

Where do you find the most fish?

Between the head and the tail.

Fractions are usually written with a **hyphen**:

Four-fifths of people understand fractions and **three-quarters** of them don't.

6 Something fishy's going on here

The Odd Mob see a sign that catches their attention.

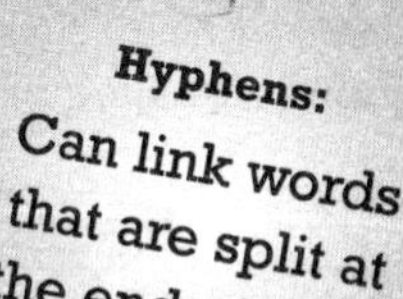

Hyphens:
Can link words that are split at the end of lines

SPECIAL ATTRACTION

Come and see the beautiful mermaid.

Only £1 to see this mysterious crea-
ture of the sea.

Don't miss this chance of a lifetime!

Whoever designed this sign hasn't done a very good job. They've had to use **hyphens** to divide the words at the end of the lines. This is allowed but it doesn't make for easy reading and you should avoid doing it if you can.

You can use a **hyphen** to divide words at the end of a line, but only make the break between syllables and not anywhere else:

Come and see the beautiful mermaid! ✓

Come and see the beautiful mermaid today! ✗

7 The Mermaid

Hyphens: Can help avoid word confusion

All is revealed.

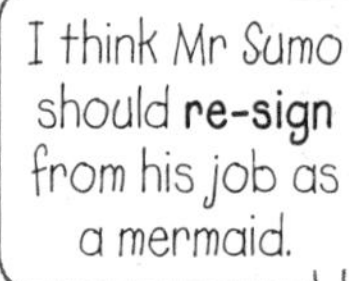

That's not a mermaid, that's Mr Sumo!
I need a lie down to **re-cover** from this horrible sight.
I think Mr Sumo should **re-sign** from his job as a mermaid.
I think you mean **recover** and **resign**.

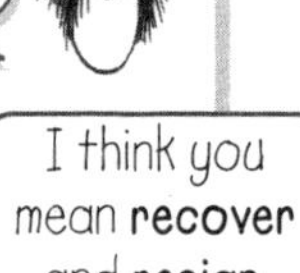

Googal's right. Wozza meant she needed to feel better again, or **recover** after the dreadful sight. To **re-cover** means to put a cover on something again (although covering up Mr Sumo with an old blanket is definitely a fine idea).

Deej meant that Mr Sumo should give up his job, or **resign**. To **re-sign** means to sign your name again and seeing Mr Sumo dressed up as a mermaid once is more than enough already!

Joke Break

Q. What goes up and down the river at 100 miles an hour?

A: A motor pike!

Use a hyphen when it can stop a word having the wrong meaning:

The fish tank was meant to be a **re-creation** (re-making) of a rock pool. ✓

The fish tank was meant to be a **recreation** (a playful activity) of a rock pool. ✗

8 The Mermaid – continued

Hyphens:
Used in ordering numbers

What a swizz! That wasn't a mermaid; it was just Mr Sumo. I want my money back.

Yeah, I want my money back too.

We do as well!

Oh no; you're the forty-seventh, forty-eighth, forty-ninth and fiftieth people to want a refund today! The aquarium's in BIG trouble now. Just wait till I get my hands on Mr Sumo!

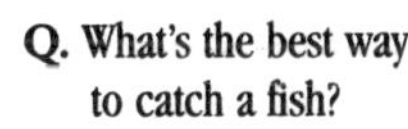

Joke Break

Q. What's the best way to catch a fish?

A: Have someone throw it to you.

Words that show the order of something use **hyphens** if the number is made of two or more words:

sixty-sixth ✓ thirty-fifth ✓ fifti-eth ✗

9 A quick recall

Hyphens link two words, e.g. man-eater.

Hyphens make meanings clear, e.g. a little-used aquarium is not the same as a little used aquarium.

Hyphens make adjectives from two words, e.g. Mr Sumo is a part-time mermaid.

Hyphens make awkward words easier to read, e.g. Sharks and pilot fish share a peaceful co-existence.

Hyphens can **di-vide** words at the end of a line.

Use hypens when writing fractions, e.g. Four-fifths of all children like dolphins.

How come these fish are so smart?

Because they hang around in schools.

The Odd Mob have had a whale of a time at the aquarium but now it's time to go.

Multiple Joyce

Which of these hyphens is correct?

A Hy-phen
B Hi-tech
C Hi-mum
D High-mum

The Ellipsis

Ellipsis:
Three dots

(1) The accident

The children are trying to spot fish in a river when something happens …

The gang are leaning over the bridge looking down into the river when there's a splash. Deej has dropped his iPod in the water! To find out what happens next you must read on …

An ellipsis is three dots in a row

An **ellipsis** is a row of **three dots** used in writing to show something is missing, or still to come:

I hope I'm going to like what's coming …

② Hanging around

The Odd Mob are in danger.

Ellipsis:
Can show an interruption

Ulf and HMD are holding Deej by his feet as he dangles over the bridge trying to reach down into the river to get his iPod back.

Be careful or you'll ...
Drop him right in it.
I've heard about splashing out ...
But this is ridiculous.

A van is hurtling towards the bridge.

That van is ...
Going way too fast.
Everybody jump before ...
It crashes into us.

The van has crashed into the bridge.

Hey, that was ...
Too close for comfort.
Still playing. I can hear it.
Yeah, but what about my iPod? It's ...

Don't tell me it's ...
Handel's Water Music!

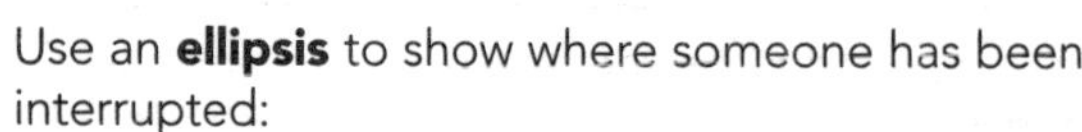

Use an **ellipsis** to show where someone has been interrupted:

Googal said, "Who's got my ..."

"I have," interrupted Flash.

3 An idea is born ... I think.

Googal's not just a pretty face.

Ellipsis:
Shows a pause

Hmm ... these sponges have given me an idea.

Ah ... I can see by those three dots that Googal is pausing to think of a way to save Deej's iPod.

Joke Break

Q. Why did the mouse take a bath?

A: To get squeaky clean.

Three dots can show the pause when someone is thinking:

"Oops ... I must have mistaken the brake for the accelerator," said the driver.

4 The sponger

Googal shocks the Odd Mob.

Ellipsis:
Needs a space at both ends

Googal had a great idea to rescue Deej's iPod. She walked over to the van ... then she reached in and grabbed an armful of sponges. We all stood and stared at her ... because ... I don't know ... we thought she'd gone mad or something.

Wozza's written about the adventure in her diary. Look how she's left a space each time before and after the three dots.

Googal ... put those sponges back.
I don't like sponges ... they remind me of bath night.

When you want to use **...** in the middle of a sentence, follow this rule:

word space **dotdotdot** space **word**

Deej had given up hope of ever seeing his iPod **again ... then** Googal had an idea.

Joke Break

Police Constable: Someone's stolen two hundred bars of soap.

Detective: Right, that tells me we're looking for a dirty thief.

(5) A sponge in time

Googal's idea isn't full of holes.

Ellipsis: What about the full stop?

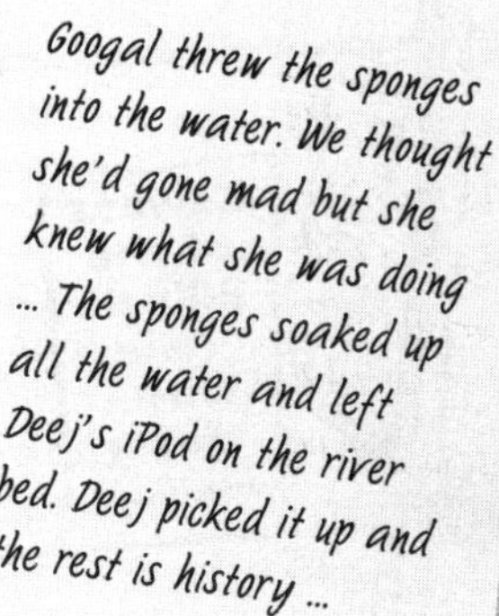

Googal threw the sponges into the water. We thought she'd gone mad but she knew what she was doing ... The sponges soaked up all the water and left Deej's iPod on the river bed. Deej picked it up and the rest is history ...

There's a first time for everything ...
You're brill. Googal. I'm lost for words ...

Wozza hasn't used a full stop after the ellipsis even though the ellipsis is at the end of the sentence. The ellipsis takes the place of the full stop.

If you end a sentence with three dots (to show a pause or passage of time) you don't need to use a full stop as well:

Googal always had the last word … The others were in awe of her brainpower.

6 A quick recall

Watch out for an ellipsis when:

- there's something left out ... where?
- there's an interruption ... what?
- there's a pause ... oh, do hurry up!

And make sure:

- there's a **space** ... **at** either end of them.
- there's no full stop before an ellipsis, not even if it comes at the end of a sentence ...

Multiple Joyce

Which of these is an ellipsis?

A Dash dash dash
B Dot dot dot
C Dot dash dot
D Morse code

Bullet Points

Getting the Bug

Bullet points: Help to set out writing

1 Creepy crawly creativity

Googal, Ulf, Deej and Wozza are doing a homework project on minibeasts. They each have to make notes about a bug they've seen.

Ulf's found a beetle in his armpit. Here are his notes:

the beetle is green and yellow
It has long antennae.
It also has a hard body
and six legs. The beetle is
about 9cm. It has wings.

He showed it to Google:

That's good, Ulf – but can you set it out better with **bullet points**?

Uhh? Can you show me please?

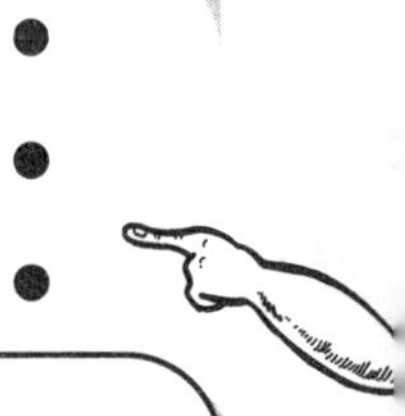

bullet points

Bullet points:

- Can help you to set out writing
- Are often used when making notes

2 Beetle mania

Googal shows Ulf how he could set out his notes about bugs.

Bullet points: Help to organise information

I found this beetle in my armpit. It has the following features:

- Green and yellow colouring
- Long antennae
- A hard body about 9cm long
- Six legs
- Wings

Thanks – that's much clearer.

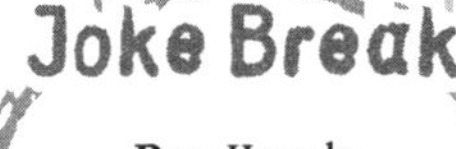

Ray: How do fleas travel?

Faye: They itch hike.

Yes, bullet points can help you to organise information in a piece of writing.

Bullet points:

- Are only one way of organising notes
- Show information in a clear way
- Act as a kind of list

③ See shell

Wozza decides to have a go at using bullet points for her minibeast homework. She shows her notes to Googal.

Bullet points: Used for brief key points

My snail

- My snail has a big brown shell which has got lots of swirly white lines on it.
- I found the snail under a big stone in my back garden. I found out that they like to live in cool damp places. They eat plants.
- I learned from the Internet that a snail's shell is for protection. Snails have soft bodies and are eaten by predators like birds.

You have some great info here, Wozza, but the bullet points aren't quite right. Each bullet point should be short, not a whole paragraph.

Try not to use too many bullet points: 6-7 is usually enough. And don't use them in stories!

What's the problem? Please show me what to do, Goog.

Bullet points:

- Are used to make short key points
- Do not usually contain long sentences
- Do not usually include whole paragraphs

Bullet points: Can shorten writing

4 Snail tale

Googal helps Wozza to use bullet points correctly in her writing.

Snails

I found a snail with a large brown and white shell under a stone in my garden. I also researched these facts about snails using the Internet:

- *Snails prefer damp, cool habitats*
- *Snails eat plants*
- *Snails have soft bodies*
- *A snail's shell is for protection*
- *Snails are eaten by predators such as birds*

Ta, Goog – that's much clearer.

Bullet points mean that you can use fewer words. They also make information stand out.

Bullet points are used for writing such as:

- Notes and lists
- Emails
- Messages

5 Soup of the day

Deej's minibeast notes are a little different ...

Bullet points:
Usually start with capitals

Leech Soup

To make fresh leech soup you need 26 fat leeches, 500ml milk and some nutmeg.

- first, put the milk in the saucepan.
- add the leeches.
- stir but do not heat.
- leave for 4 days.
- add nutmeg and serve.

Deej, that's truly disgusting. And it should be a numbered list anyway. The punctuation is a bit iffy too.

Hey, that's an old family recipe! Please explain about the numbering though.

House fly

Bullet points:

- Usually start with a capital letter
- Do not usually end with a full stop
- Do have full stops if sentences are used

Bullet points: Numbers are used for sequences

6 Order, please!

Googal explains to Deej that numbers or letters are used instead of bullets where the order is important. She shows him an example:

Life Cycle of the Butterfly

1. An adult butterfly lays eggs.
2. The eggs hatch into larvae (caterpillars).
3. Each larva forms a hard shell called a pupa.
4. Inside the pupa the larva changes into a butterfly.
5. The adult butterfly emerges.

A life cycle is an example of a **sequence**. Instructions and recipes are sequences too – the order is important.
I see – so that's why numbers are used instead of bullets. Now, how about some butterfly soup?

Numbers or **letters** can be used instead of bullets where the **order** is important.

1. first
2. next
3. finally

7 A quick recall

Use **bullet points** to:

- Outline key points in writing
- Organise information
- Make a list stand out
- Keep notes brief

Multiple Joyce

Bullet points should be used to

A Draw attention
B Draw a picture
C Fire the imagination
D Shoot a script

Wozza! I found a huge minibeast with black leathery skin and five legs. And I lost my glasses.

You'd better find those specs. That's a glove ...

The Forward Slash

Rounders Bout

The forward slash:
Shows alternatives

1 Completely batty

The Odd Mob decide to enter a rounders tournament. Googal is reading the rules.

It says that each player must provide his/her own bat.

What if he/she has only got a manky one?

Then he/she had better borrow one from a brother/sister/friend!

The forward slash can sometimes be used instead of the word 'or' where there are alternatives:

his/her means his **or** her

sister/brother means sister **or** brother

/

a forward slash

The **forward slash**, **or stroke**, can be used instead of the word '**or**':

he/she = he or she

② Bust to the game

The gang are travelling to the tournament – definitely not in style ...

The forward slash:
Can be used instead of 'and'

The Essex/Kent border means the border between Essex **and** Kent.

The fuel used by the bus was a petrol/vinegar mix (a mixture of petrol **and** vinegar).

A **forward slash** can sometimes be used instead of the word '**and**':

an on/off switch = an on **and** off switch

③ The big one

The kids finally arrive at the tournament, after walking most of the way.

Their first game is against Treatment RC.

The forward slash:
Can show a period of time

I heard that this team hasn't been beaten since 1962/63.

I reckon that's because no one survived to tell the tale ...

The forward slash is used to show a length of time:

The Odd Mob were training in April/May (April to May) – far too late!

Joke Break

Ray: What's a wombat for?

Faye: Playing wom.

The **forward slash** can show a **period of time**:
2007/8 = 2007 to 2008

4 Ballistic bowling

Oh no! It turns out that Mr Sumo plays for the opposition – and he's bowling.

The first six Odd Mob players are out first ball …

The forward slash:
Used in some units of measurement

Yikes! That ball must be travelling at 600km/h!
We're doomed!

A forward slash is sometimes used instead of the word '**per**' in a speed or other scientific measurement.

600km**/**h means 600 kilometres **per** hour.

Cheesy Chad says ...

Km/h is sometimes written as kph.

Speed measurements can be shown using a **forward slash**:

2 m**/**s = 2 metres per second.

(5) Flashtastic!

The forward slash:
Used to show fractions

It looks like Mr Sumo is going to beat the gang on his own, but he hasn't counted on Flash.

Eh? Where did she go?

Flash has scored 1/2 a rounder!

A forward slash is sometimes used to show fractions:

1/2 means half.

Rounder player

Fractions can be written with a **forward slash**:
3/4 = $\frac{3}{4}$ 7/8 = $\frac{7}{8}$

6 Out cold!

The forward slash:
Used for some abbreviations

Flash scores $688\frac{1}{2}$ rounders for the Odd Mob. Next, it's the other team's turn to bat …

Well caught, Shagpile!
But where's Mr Sumo?

It turns out that Mr Sumo fainted trying to bowl out Flash. He was taken to hospital, so the Odd Mob wrote him a 'get well soon' card:

Mr Sumo
c/o The Rotund Wrestlers' Hospital
Bellytown,
Beds.

Notice the stroke on the address? c/o means 'care of'.

A **stroke** can be used to **abbreviate** a word or phrase:
A/c = account   R/C = radio control

(7) A quick recall

Well, in the end, the rounders match is a $688\frac{1}{2} - 688\frac{1}{2}$ draw, so everyone goes home happy, except Mr Sumo, whose right arm is now 17cm longer than his left …

A forward slash can be used:

- Instead of 'or' (eg his/her)
- Instead of 'and' (eg Essex/Kent border)
- To show a period of time (eg 1962/3)
- Instead of 'per' in a unit of measurement (eg 100 km/h)
- To write a fraction (eg 3/4)
- In an abbreviation (eg c/o)

Multiple Joyce

What does b/g usually stand for?

A Background
B Big granny
C Britain's Great
D Beautiful gravy

It's best to avoid using the forward slash in formal writing if you can.

Italics, Bold and Underlining

Are You All right, Pet?

Italics, bold and underlining:
For highlighting text

1 The pet shop boys

Ulf has saved up enough money to buy himself a new pet. Deej is helping him find a good shop.

The Orange Pages have an advert here for Pete's Perilous Pets.

Pete's Perilous Pets

For all your dangerous, deadly and large animal requirements

<u>Poisonous killers our speciality</u>

53, The High St. Tel 448762

italics

bold

<u>underlining</u>

Did you notice how some words in the advert are **bold**, some are <u>underlined</u> and some are *italic*? This is to help you notice them.

Italics, **bold** and <u>underlining</u> are used to highlight printed text.

2 The bear facts

Italics, bold and underlining:
Used for foreign words

Ulf and Deej visit Pete's pet shop to see if there is anything interesting.

What do you stock?
We have vipers, crocs, tigers, scorpions, tarantulas, sharks and so on.
Have you got anything for under £1?
There's a special offer on grizzly bears at the moment: two for 99p.
PET

Great – I'll take three!
Grizzly bear
Ursus arctos

The Latin name for the grizzly bear is written in *italics* on the cage. Foreign words are also sometimes written in *italics*.

Latin words and **foreign** words are often written in *italics*:

Ciao: Italian for 'hello' and 'goodbye'

RSVP (*Respondez s'il vous plait:*) French for 'please reply'

3 The bear necessities

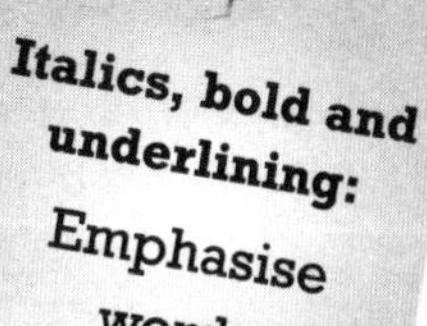

Ulf takes the bears home. Pete the pet shop owner has given him a leaflet about looking after them.

Caring for your Grizzly

<u>WARNING:</u>

Never put your head in a grizzly's mouth if you want it back.

The word 'warning' is underlined. This is because it is important. Important words in printed text are often underlined, written in bold, or in capitals.

Joke Break

Al: Why do bears have fur coats?

Eli: Cos they'd look stupid in parkas.

Bold and underlining is used to emphasise important words:

Danger! <u>Keep out</u> **Important notice**

4 Grizzly grub

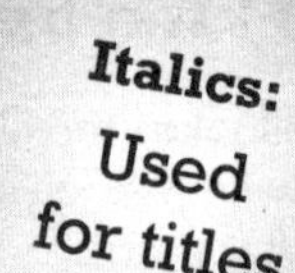

Deej calls Ulf to see how he is getting on with his new pets.

How are the bears, Ulf?
They've eaten well. First they ate the furniture, then they ate the garden. All of it. They're tired now – I think they want a story.

Deej did some web research and printed out a list of suitable story books to email to Ulf:

Winnie the Pooh
Paddington Bear
The Rupert Bear Annual
Teddy Robinson

Titles of books, films, plays etc are often written in italics:
Old Bear *The Little Polar Bear*

5 A fairytale ending

It looks like Ulf has already found the perfect story ...

Italics:
Used for quotations

Once upon a time, there was a little girl called Goldilocks.

Then the bears finished off the day by eating cold porridge, breaking some chairs and sleeping in Ulf's bed.

Cheesy Chad says ...

Italics, bold and underlining are mainly used when writing on a computer.

Quotations are sometimes written in *italics* instead of using quotation marks:

The End

⑥ Ulf warning

The next day, Ulf takes the three bears back to the pet shop. It turns out they were too scared of him.

When to use italics, bold and underlining:

- To emphasise words so that they stand out:

  <u>Beware</u> of the bears

- Italics are used to write some foreign or Latin words:

  Ursus arctos

- Italics can be used to write titles of books, films, plays, etc:

  Goldilocks and the Three Bears

- Italics are also used to write quotations. As Ulf said: *I see why he was called Winnie the Pooh now.*

Multiple Joyce

Which of these uses italics correctly?

A Grrr, *went* the bear.
B Grrr, went the *bear*.
C *Grrr*, went the bear.
D *Grrr, went Ulf*.

Numbers and Figures

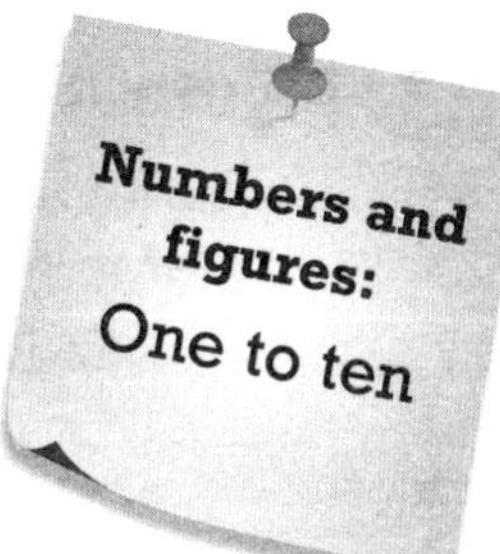

I-Spy

1 The secret seven

One day, a mysterious woman arrives at Googal's house.

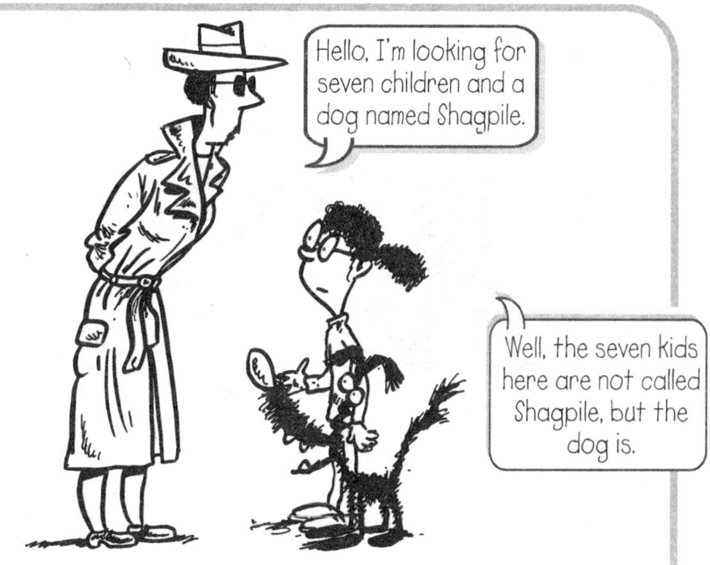

Hello, I'm looking for seven children and a dog named Shagpile.

Well, the seven kids here are not called Shagpile, but the dog is.

The woman shows Googal some ID. She is from the Secret Service!

Notice how it says '**seven** children' above, and not '7 children'.

The **numbers** from one to ten are usually written as **words** in a piece of writing:

I saw three ships. ✓ I saw 3 ships. ✗

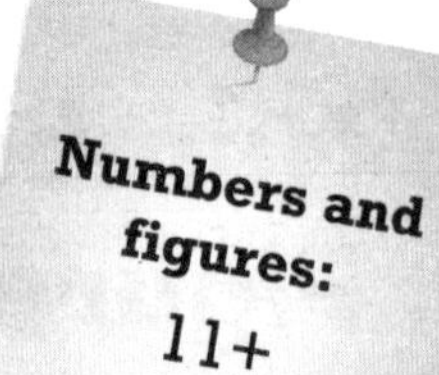

② Figure it out

Once inside, the secret agent tells the gang some interesting information.

We've been watching the house at 86 Mighty Close. Over 530 mysterious parcels have been delivered there in the last 12 days.

Hey – I know that house! It's near number 85.

In the speech bubbles above, 86, 530 and 85 are written as **figures** because they are over **ten**.

Numbers above **ten** are usually written as **figures**:

11 38 17,392

③ Watch it!

Numbers and figures: Writing numbers

The kids are baffled as to why the secret agent is telling them all this.

Twenty-four is written in figures above because it follows 86. It is confusing to write them both as figures.

Avoid using two sets of figures next to each other in a sentence:

In 2006 10 prisoners escaped. ✗

In 2006 ten prisoners escaped. ✓

Numbers and figures:
Starting with numbers

4 Barking mad

The secret agent then takes them to the house they have to watch.

Twenty-four hours is a long time, so you'd better split up into groups of two and do six hours each.

Six hours sounds OK, if we have four groups of two. Shagpile, bark once if you agree and twice if not.

Woof, woof, woof!

Joke Break

Az: Were you long at the doctors?

Baz: No, the same size as I am now.

A number **starting** a sentence is usually written in **words**:

60 minutes seems likes hours to Ulf. ✗

Sixty minutes seems like hours to Ulf. ✓

Numbers and figures:
Writing dates

(5) A date with destiny

Flash and Max volunteer to spy on the house first. The secret agent tells them to take notes.

Are you sure we look normal?

Here are their notes:

Date:

~~July 23, 2010~~

~~23 July, 2010~~

~~July 23rd 2010~~

~~23rd July '10~~

~~23.7.10~~

23/07/10

Yikes! There was no room to write anything else because Max wasn't sure how to write the **date**. Actually, all of the versions above are OK!

There are many ways to write the **date**:

13.11.12 Nov 13th 2012 13 November '12

6 Oh year

Numbers and figures:
Periods of time

Nothing much happened outside the house at first, then Googal and Deej take a turn at the undercover work.

Look! A car is pulling up.

Yes! It's stopping too.

Here are their notes:

Date: 23.7.10
Time 7.02 am.
A green Ferrari estate stops outside the house. Registration IFF 1 E (that's 1997–8).
A man gets out wearing a 70s soul outfit from the late 20th Century. He takes a parcel to the house.

Notice how Googal refers to periods of time three different ways.

There are several ways to refer to a **period of time**:

35 BC ✓ 1939–1945 ✓ 2006/7 ✓ 1990s ✓ 50s ✓
19th Century ✓ 200 AD ✓ 1983–84 ✓ 1999–01 ✗
1750's ✗ 60's ✗ 21 Century ✗

7 Time for action

Numbers and figures: Writing times

HMD and Wozza take over the spying duties just before midday. Things begin to hot up ...

More deliveries!
Hee hee – they'll never suspect we're watching them.
SPY KIT

Here are their notes:

Date: 23rd July 2006
11.53 am – four parcels arrive
12.00 midday – one parcel
12.20 pm – 12 parcels
1:30 pm – three parcels
14:40 – two parcels

Cheesy Chad says ...

Times are usually written with am (before midday) or pm (after midday).

HMD and Wozza write the time several different ways – each is correct. It's a pity they don't notice who's answering the door ...

There are several ways to write **times of day**:
10.00 am ✓ 12.00 midnight ✓ 4:33 pm ✓ 20:00 ✓
6.20 ✗ (no **am** or **pm**)

8 Taking ages

Numbers and figures: Writing ages

Finally, Ulf and Shagpile take over the late shift, watching the mysterious house at 86 Mighty Close.

You write the notes, Shagpile. I'll drop this rock on anyone suspicious.

Here are their notes (dog-eared!):

Date: yes
A large 33-year-old man took delivery of seven parcels.
Ulf knocked out a delivery driver who was in her forties.

Joke Break

Prisoner: I'm free! I'm free!

Little kid: So what, I'm four.

Notice how the ages of the two people are written.

People's **ages** can be written in several ways:
He is aged 12 ✓ An 18-year-old ✓
A man in his sixties ✓

9 Order, order!

The next day, the secret agent returns to see what the Odd Mob have found out.

Numbers and figures: Writing order

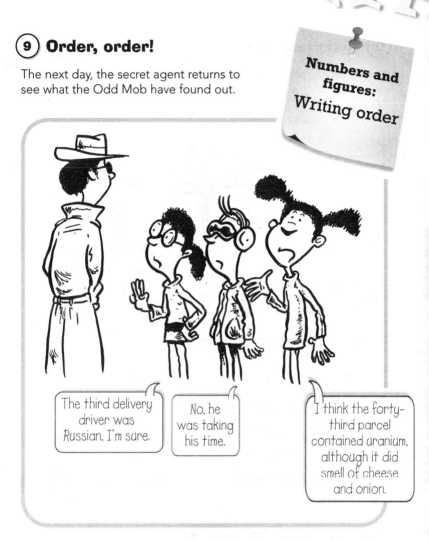

The third delivery driver was Russian, I'm sure.

No, he was taking his time.

I think the forty-third parcel contained uranium, although it did smell of cheese and onion.

Words that show the **order** of something are called ordinal numbers, e.g. first, second, third. They are usually written in letters up to ninety-nine and then in figures.

Ordinal numbers are usually written like this:

second eighth ninety-first 200th

(10) Fraction friction

Numbers and figures: Writing fractions

The secret agent is losing patience with the gang.

You've been yakking for three-quarters of an hour! And you still haven't told me who lives at number 86.

Oh, that's easy – we saw him half a dozen times. It's Mr Sumo.

Silly woman – I've been woofing that for two-thirds of the day ...

So, it's the kids' old enemy who is taking in the mysterious parcels. But look at the way that the three fractions are written above.

Some **fractions** are written with a **hyphen**:
two-fifths   nine-tenths   <u>but</u> one eighth

(11) Pie spy

Numbers and figures: Writing money

So, what is it that Mr Sumo is having delivered to his house? Jewels? Stolen goods? Counterfeit DVDs? A police raid is organised.

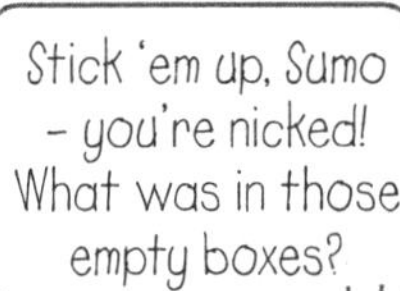

Stick 'em up, Sumo – you're nicked! What was in those empty boxes?

It was my lunch, that's all. I have about 27 pies a day. It only costs me £1,600 a month.

Cheesy Chad says ...

Very large amounts of money (e.g. over a million pounds) are often written in words instead of figures.

So, that's it, just some unhealthy munching! Googal calculates that, in his lifetime, Mr Sumo has already spent £3.9m on pie-based snacking!

Money can be written in several ways:

3p   £2.50   £80,000 $1m   four billion Euros

<u>but</u> £4,876,000

(12) A quick recall

Well, spying hasn't been as much fun as the gang thought it would be. And it's put them off pies for life …

A few things to remember:

- Write the numbers one to ten as words
- Write numbers above ten as figures
- Avoid writing two sets of figures together in a sentence
- Try not to start sentences with figures
- There are many ways to write periods of time
- Times of day are usually written with am or pm
- Many fractions have hyphens when written as words
- Very large numbers are often written as words

Multiple Joyce

Which of these is not a date?

A 28th August 1534
B 1/1/00
C 3rd September 1988
D Ulf going out with Flash

It's put me off too.

Index

Multiple Joyce answers

page 16	Capital letters – A
page 25	Full stops – D
page 35	Exclamation marks – C
page 51	Semicolons – A
page 57	Colons – A
page 64	Quotation marks – C
page 72	Punctuating direct speech – A
page 80	Apostrophes – A
page 87	Brackets – A
page 95	Dashes – A
page 104	Hyphens – B
page 110	The Ellipsis – B
page 117	Bullet Points – A
page 124	The Forward Slash – A
page 130	Italics, Bold and Underlining – C
page 142	Numbers and Figures – D